Shifting Winds

Nebraska's Weather Story

Shifting Winds

Nebraska's Weather Story

by Betty Stevens

Published 1994 by Journal-Star Printing Co.

With the exception of materials provided by the Nebraska State Historical Society, all the photographs reprinted in this volume were taken from the library files of the Lincoln Journal-Star.

Library of Congress Cataloging-in-Publication Data

SHIFTING WINDS/Betty Stevens
p. cm.
ISBN 0-9638025-1-8
1. Weather — Nebraska. 2. History — Nebraska.
I. Stevens, Betty. II. Title
1994 94-75396
First Edition

Printing in the United States of America
by
BookCrafters Chelsea, Michigan

Maps and Graphics by Thomas Patrick
Cover Photo by Randy Hampton
Cover Design by Brian Noonan

CONTENTS

TED KIRK/Lincoln Journal-Star

FOREWORD

Her moods swing like those of a petulant mistress.

She draws her energy from the very forces that strike her — from arctic gales out of Canada and sultry blasts from the Gulf of Mexico, from her proximity to the Rocky Mountains and her isolation on the wide, flat prairie. She flirts ceaselessly with the jet stream but courts no body of water that might temper her wildness.

She may provide a perfect day or two, lulling even the wariest of old-timers, but she can turn in a minute to blow you away, strike you down with a bolt of lightning, drown you or drive you to distraction from a lack of rainfall. When she shakes the last spring snow from her petticoats, she can bring the experienced or the novice to a complete standstill with equal surprise.

Any year is a good year to write her biography, but 1993 is better than good. She excelled at bashing records: The third snowiest January, the coldest September; precipitation ahead of normal by May, 3 inches ahead by July and 13 inches ahead by August; floods swirling everywhere; a final trace of snow on April Fool's Day. On Oct. 6, she brought Valentine, Grand Island and North Platte recording-breaking highs of 96 degrees, 90 degrees and 91 degrees, respectively. But on Nov. 25 — Thanksgiving Day — the low of 5 degrees broke all records on a day when the state high reached a mere 18. Then she finished out the year with the third coldest autumn on record.

Her name is Nebraska Weather. Volumes could be written. This is only a sample of her story.

— Betty Stevens
March 15, 1994

ROBERT BECKER/Lincoln Journal-Star

DROUGHTS

"My theory is that rain means more on the Plains than it does elsewhere. Where there is plenty of rain, everyone expects it; where there is no rain, no one expects it; but all across the Dakotas, Nebraska, Kansas, Oklahoma, Texas and the Plains areas of the West, rain is not a statement, yes or no, but a question. It was here that the settlers entered the marginal farming lands and began to beg for rain on a regular basis."

— Roger L. Welsch
The Summer It Rained

1988's summer drought finally was broken by rains in the spring of 1989, but Nebraska farmers still faced a challenge: waiting for their once-parched fields to dry enough for planting to begin, as on this farm northwest of Lincoln.

2 SHIFTING WINDS

DROUGHTS

Keith Church slightly narrows his bright blue eyes — the better to draw a bead on the past.

He's 76 now, and as if it were yesterday he recalls those tragic days in the 1930s when he was in his middle and late teens and a drought sucked the life out of the soil, the livestock and finally the people themselves.

To set the comparative stage for that weather tragedy of 60 years ago, Church talks about World War II, when he was an Army infantryman in a combat unit: "It was kill or be killed, and I can think of at least a dozen times when I might have died. But that was not as stressful as the depression and drought of the 1930s. The '30s toughened me up for combat and for the rest of my life," he said.

Nebraska was included in the 65 percent of the nation that was experiencing severe or extreme drought during that decade. In both 1934 and 1936, rainfall amounted to less than 15 inches — less than half the annual average of more than 30 inches.

Church lived with his family on a quarter-section near Bennet. "You couldn't get a hold of neither a job nor a dollar. Half of Bennet was for sale for back taxes. A really good house could have been bought for $1,000 and a 160-acre farm for $2,000."

Because of chickens, cows and hogs that the Churches kept alive on failed crops that would not sell — plus a kitchen garden — "we had a good table. Our livin' came right out of the cellar."

Church remembers: "Doc Cameron charged $1.50 for house calls. If there was no money to pay him, he took an old setting hen or a pint of cream." And if Church's friends could pool a few pennies for gasoline, a big Saturday night could be purchased in the Capital City for 25 cents. "A hamburger was a dime, the movie a dime and a bag of popcorn was a nickel," he recalled.

"At the end of the '30s, when I finally got a job with the railroad for 35 cents an hour, I thought I was flying with the geese. It all taught me a lesson I never forgot." Church worked for 32 years as a security officer with FirsTier in Lincoln because the job was steady. "You couldn't have driven me away from there with a bullwhip. To this day, when I get a dollar, I immediately start figuring out where the next one is coming from.".

"Nobody who lived through it will forget the drought of the 1930s," said Don Wilhite, a meteorologist at the University of Nebraska-Lincoln and director of the International Drought Information Center.

Drought is a natural phenomenon that needs to be thought of in an international setting, he said.

That's true, meteorologically speaking, but when drought has oven-baked the soil so that seeds sown will not germinate but only lie there, or when rain does not fall prior to and during that critical period when the corn is tasseling, then drought's dry and bony fingers are picking a lot of pockets in Nebraska. It seems more like a personal assault than a natural phenomenon.

While there are dozens of definitions for what constitutes a drought, one is such a deficiency of precipitation from what is expected over a short or longer period of time that it is not sufficient to meet the demands of human activities. "The magnitude of impact is related to the onset of the lack of precipitation, its intensity and duration," Wilhite said.

The drought of the '30s was 60 years ago, so the number of people who had an adult and first-hand experience with those Dust Bowl years is diminishing rapidly. But there were people who recorded that unbelievable hardship so that it would be remembered forever. Hallie Meyers Nelson was one of them.

She was a farm wife who lived with her husband, Jim, near Broken Bow. Writing about the summer of 1934, Nelson recorded in her book, *South of the Cottonwood Tree:* "On May 6 the thermometer on the north side of the house registered 106 degrees. The hot south wind made the heat seem more unbearable."

The thermomenter registered 117 degrees at noon the day the Nelsons' third son was born on July 8, 1934. That was the same year the federal government initiated a program administered by county extension agents that paid farmers for livestock for which they had no feed. Payments ranged from $6 for cattle 2 years old and older down to $1 for calves less than a year old.

The temperature soared over 100 degrees on 22 days in 1934, and in 1936 baked Nebraska with 18 days of 100-degree-plus temperatures. Lincoln's

Journal-Star Files

A Nebraska farmer surveys a fence buried by drifting sand during the Dust Bowl days of the 1930s.

hottest day on record still is July 25, 1936; the mercury climbed to 115 degrees. The next day, 24 weather stations in the state recorded temperatures even higher. There were 4,500 deaths blamed on the heat during that one month nationwide.

Nelson wrote of 1935: "As spring advanced, the temperatures rose. Still there was no rainfall of any consequence. Farmers plowed or disked the dry fields, hoping rain would come before planting time. The vicious winds blew the topsoil up in clouds. Crops were again planted in dry soil. In places the corn or grain came up. A few light showers kept it alive for a time, but by mid-summer everyone knew there would be no crops again this year.

"Cream and eggs were our only source of steady income. Market price for eggs was around 9 cents a dozen. One of the hottest days of that summer, Jim took a load of eggs and cream to town. The temperature was near 115 degrees by midafternoon. When he came home that evening he brought the eggs back. The produce store refused to buy them because of the heat.

The produce dealer broke an egg in a small dish. The yolk had become so warm it had broken and spread through the white."

The eggs were fed to the Nelsons' hogs.

"We heard reports that livestock was dying because of the unbearable heat," she wrote. "Chickens fell off the roosts, dead. Horses and cattle were found dead in the pastures where there was no shade. Hogs died by the score.

"When all the loose Nebraska dust was blown away, it began to blow in from Kansas, Oklahoma and Texas. . . . In a short time, everything — building roofs, bushes, weeds, garden plants and even the cat and dog were layered with the red dust of Oklahoma and Texas."

Of the heat, Nelson wrote: "We laid three or four foot-wide boards about eight feet long between two sawhorses and slept outside until midnight or later. In cities, people were sleeping on lawns."

That was true in the Capital City, where night after night in those pre-air-conditioning days the lawn of the state Capitol was covered with Lincolnites trying to find a spot cool enough to allow sleep.

Nelson included in her story a J.C. Penney advertisement published in the Custer County Chief on June 20, 1938, as a demonstration of how the drought had affected prices: Boys' Oxhide overalls, 43 cents; men's Big Mac overalls, 89 cents; ladies' shoes, 98 cents; men's suede leather jackets, $4.98; sheet blankets, 59 cents. From a Safeway ad, Jan. 20, 1940: two pounds of sugar, 15 cents; grapefruit, 25 cents a dozen; 24-ounce loaves of bread,

Journal-Star Files

Years of drought had left this Neligh farm desolate by 1938.

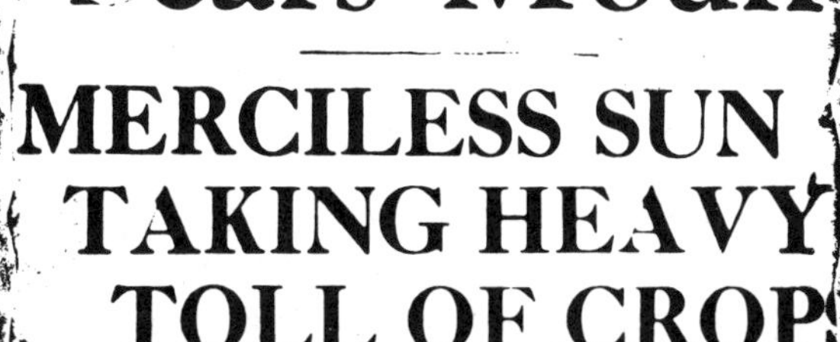

MERCILESS SUN TAKING HEAVY TOLL OF CROP

Monday Mercury Seems Bent On Vieing F
Lincoln's All-Tim
Set Sunday

HOTTEST WEEK IN HISTORY OF CITY CLOSES; NO LETUP

2 Additional Heat Deaths Make 12 Since Midweek; 107 Again Here.

CONTINUED 'WARM' SUNDAY

CLOUDY SKIES FAIL TO HALT MERCURY RISE

Highest Minimum Ever Recorded Here Set Friday Morning.

MERCURY ABOVE 85 ALL NIGHT

Weather Bureau Predicts Thunderstorms For Lincoln Area.

116 AT BEATRICE

BEATRICE, Neb., July 13—
time heat record of a frac-
degrees was estab-
p. m. today and
was still
rd was 112
is year and

reached
the nine-
that the
The

FIVE VICTIMS REPORTED IN LINCOLN ARE

Tenth Consecutive Day of Above 100 De
Heat Blisters City and State — T
Women Stricken Here, and Death Repo
at Valparaiso and Union.

Journal-Star Files

Headlines collected from Lincoln newspapers published in July 1934, indicate the effects of the searing heatwave.

two for 15 cents.

Even at those prices, who could buy? Farmers were getting 6 to 8 cents a pound for hogs, 10 cents for a pound of butterfat, 10 to 15 cents a bushel for corn, and weaned calves weighing between 300 and 400 pounds sold for $6 or $8 each.

"I wondered if we weren't foolhardy to refuse to give up," Nelson wrote, reflecting the agonizing decision with which thousands of Nebraskans wrestled daily. "Only those who lived through that period of history can realize the mental anguish and physical punishment which nagged us constantly. No one knew which way to turn or what to do. Each family had to fend for themselves. Neighbors were always willing to help with work, but almost no one had any money.

"Perhaps it was sheer stubbornness that we so tenaciously hung on and kept trying, determined to demonstrate to our neighbors and our families that we hadn't lost faith in Nebraska or ourselves."

In Nebraska — and other predominately farming states — drought is thought of as an agricultural deficit, Wilhite wrote in *Encyclopedia of Earth System Science, Vol. II,* but other types are meteorological, hydrological and socioeconomic.

Meteorological drought is expressed solely on the degree of dryness and must be viewed from a regional point of view, Wilhite explained. Hydrological droughts are concerned with the effects of periods of precipitation shortfalls on surface or subsurface water supplies.

"Meteorological droughts result from precipitation deficiencies, while agricultural droughts are largely the result of soil moisture deficiences. More time elapses before precipitation deficiencies show up in components of the hydrological system. As a result, impacts are out of phase with those in other economic sectors."

The frequency and severity of hydrological drought is often defined in terms of its influence on river basins. Socioeconomic drought is demonstrated by the relationship between drought and human activities, such as poor land practices that lead to soil erosion, enhancing the vulnerability to future droughts.

Droughts also differ in three essential characteristics: intensity, the degree of precipitation shortfall; duration, usually requiring a minimum of two to three months to become established but then possibly continuing for years; and spatial coverage, the geographical area affected.

Most Nebraskans know how drought affects agricultural production, but it is difficult to find any area of economic, environmental and social life that escapes. Some less obvious costs that can be attributed to drought include damage to fish and wildlife species, danger from range and forest fires, additional cost of water transport or transfer, loss of revenue related

Nebraska State Historical Society

Drought relief supplies arrive in Elm Creek in 1894.

to recreational activities, tree disease and insect infestation.

Like other long-held legends about weather in this state, the relationship of grasshopper infestation to droughts is very much up in the air and may slide entirely out the window. The idea that they are related has been around since the last century, and some researchers still promulgate that idea. But University of Nebraska-Lincoln biology professor Anthony Joern, the only grasshopper ecologist in the state, said: "The real data demonstrates a very weak relationship between drought and grasshopper infestations. What may really happen is that during a drought there is not much plant material and consequently grasshoppers are noticed more. When it's hot and dry, we see lots of grasshoppers. When the foliage is lush, there may be just as many but we don't notice them."

In fact, some researchers elsewhere have found that the grasshopper population sometimes is diminished during droughts because there is not enough foliage to sustain them.

"We're throwing the old rules out and still fighting about it," Joern said.

Nebraska State Historical Society

Lincoln experienced some of its worst dust storms in years when a drought hit Nebraska in 1950.

"It's a lot more complex than we thought."

Additional myths include where tornadoes and lightning strike or don't strike and what's true and maybe not true about the greenhouse effect.

Wilhite said that literature was full of references showing how extended periods of drought have resulted in food supply disruptions, famine, massive migrations of people and wars. In the United States, the drought of the 1930s significantly altered the settlement of the West.

So did another drought 40 years earlier.

The first Nebraska settlers already had wrestled with and lost to grasshoppers, hailstorms and prairie fires, but all those battles seemed like tea parties compared to the drought that began in 1890 and seemed to go for the jugular in 1894.

Nebraska historian A.E. Sheldon wrote of July 26, 1894: "A furnace wind began to blow from the southeast. In three days, the Nebraska corn crop was dead in the furrows." And a story in the Lincoln Journal on July 8, 1970, written about Waverly's centennial, told the story of August Brandeen, who started out from Plattsmouth through a lush, green countryside and by the time he got to Waverly, both the crops and tree leaves were so dry they could be crumpled in the hand as though a hard frost had hit them.

Faced with total crop loss, farmers had to sell or mortgage their properties and livestock. Winter became a test of fortitude, with many settlers leaving the state — or dying here.

Wilhite said that unlike other weather extremities, the media tend to ignore droughts because their impact is more subtle than, say, a tornado. Droughts do not garner the same respect because the onset is not so evident. "It is a creeping phenomenon, making its onset and end difficult to determine," he wrote.

The ripple effects of a drought make it difficult to add up the costs, but those cost do ripple. In agricultural states, when crops fail, that failure is felt in the grocery store, the bank, the implement store — there is no escape.

While droughts may not be as exciting to reporters as other weather stories, the drought of the 1890s used a lot of ink. Much of it was not entirely accurate, as many newspaper editors were committed to their bullishness on Nebraska in spite of evidence that far more people had been dried out and were leaving than were coming in. Thirty-five of Nebraska's then 90 counties lost population between 1890 and 1900. A sign often seen on wagons headed east read: "In God We Trusted. In Nebraska We Busted."

Even for the most entrenched optimists, reality became hard to ignore. After that "awful holocaust that shriveled cornblades in the blast like grass in an oven," the Axtell Republican estimated 10,000 people left Nebraska that summer. The Minden Courier reported that horses were being slaughtered in Hamilton County because there was no feed for them and they could not be given away. And in *Conquering The Great American Desert,* Everett Dick related the story of a man who shipped a carload of hogs to Kansas City in September, but learned that after the commission man had disposed of them, the sale price would not pay the freight.

The Omaha World-Herald published a series of 15 articles in the fall of 1894 with headlines like these: "Farmers Freezing and Famishing," "Eating Prairie Dogs," "Women and Children In Calico and Rags Without Shoes or Stockings in Despair."

Those articles piqued the interest of the Eastern press, and Joseph Pulitzer, publisher of the New York World, sent crack reporter Elizabeth Cochrane, who wrote under the pseudonym Nellie Blye, to Nebraska to bring back the facts. Blye, of *Around The World In 80 Days* fame, already had an international reputation.

The five stories she wrote between Jan. 28 and Feb., 13, 1895, described unbelievably harsh conditions. She advised her readers who were prone to Christian charity to forget Africa and India. There was no greater need worldwide than in rural Nebraska, Blye wrote.

As a result of her advice, barrels of donated clothing arrived from the East — although they were filled with outdated and totally inappropriate garb. One could occasionally see a weatherbeaten woman carrying water to her drought-stricken garden and wearing a taffeta party dress. A farmer was spotted plowing his fields, wearing pointed, yellow shoes.

Blye left Valentine on her first sortie into rural Nebraska, where the dust came over the hubs of the wagon wheels. "I could see for miles, but not a single sign of life, man, beast or plant met my gaze. Trees there were none." Checking soddy after abandoned soddy, Blye finally came upon a settler to interview. This farmer told her he had planted six bushels of seed potatoes and harvested one bushel in return. He planted 96 acres of corn and did not reap a single ear.

The sorrel team that pulled Blye's buggy out of Butte turned silver-white from dust. She found sodhouse dwellers trying to exist on a diet of nothing but flour and water. "Never in the history of this country has their been so much sickness. . . . The doctor said it is from insufficient food. . . . If these people were Easterners, they would have died long ago, but these inhabitants are like their horses — they can last a long time on fresh air," Blye wrote.

She found a relief commission organized at the state level for which the Legislature had appropriated $100,000. But that was very reluctant funding because legislators, like newspaper editors, hoped to keep Nebraska's dry and dirty secret from becoming public nationwide. "It was all very well to talk about droughty Kansas and suffering Dakota, but it would never do to

ROBERT BECKER/Lincoln Journal-Star

When drought struck Nebraska in 1988, this farm pond northwest of Branched Oak Lake became a puddle.

publish the fact that Nebraska was in need of help," Dick wrote in *Conquering the Great American Desert.*

Blye reported the relief effort seemed to stockpile supplies in Lincoln and Omaha, but because of bureacratic bungling — as well as unrealistic hopes and a lack of plans for delivery — few of life's necessities were getting to the people in the most desperate straits. "The starving cows, chickens and hogs have been eaten up and there are thousands of Nebraskans who must be fed until next September," Blye wrote.

Even that was optimistic. That drought, like many others, was not a single-year event.

The next year, 1895, relatives of Nebraska author Willa Cather wrote a series of letters from Webster County that were sent to the family matriarch, Caroline Cather, who was visiting the East Coast.

■ May 10, from Kyd Clutter: "Dear Grandma, things look gloomy here at present, it being rather dry. It looks like another failure and farmers are very discouraged."

■ May 22, from Franc Cather: "Dear Mother, it is getting very dry and it has been very cold. Oats and rye are suffering. Some pieces are too far gone for rain to help."

■ May 22, from Jennie Cather: "I have little news to tell except dry, dust and no rain. Everyone is low-spirited and it looks as if the good Lord has forgotten us entirely."

Things became so desperate that Nebraskans turned both to the Almighty and to rainmakers for relief. "In the Panhandle of the northwest section of the state, the 'Rain God Association' was formed in 1894 to raise $1,000 to buy gunpowder. From Long Pine to Harrison on a hot July day, on high peaks known as 'Rain God Stations,' at the arranged second, gunpowder was discharged in a steady cannonade. No rain fell, however," Louise Pound wrote in *Roundup: A Nebraska Reader.* Two Lincoln physicians were bombarding the sky with gunpowder shot from funnel-shaped cannons, and there were other efforts designed to create rain — or bamboozle the populace.

In *Conquering the Great American Desert,* Dick wrote: "The most natural thing for religious people to do was to meet at the church and pray for rain. No doubt this was done in many places, although the few newspaper references we have report only efforts where success crowned the prayers of the suppliants. In other words, prayer was only news when rain followed."

Droughts follow no pattern; they are not predictable: 1858-1866, 1880s, 1893-1895, 1910-1915, 1931-1940, 1952-1957, 1963, 1974, 1988.

Larry Weakley, a U.S. Department of Agriculture soil scientist who lived in Lincoln, became internationally known after he initiated a system of measuring droughts by the width of tree rings. His widely published findings 30 years ago provided evidence that in the 748 years previous to his study, there were 21 droughts that lasted five years or longer, spaced an average of 23.9 years apart. During 269 years of the 748-year study period, or 36 percent of the time, it was sufficiently dry to adversely affect crop production.

The University of Arizona's Tree-Ring Research Laboratory continues to study tree ring widths in relation to drought. But that is after the fact. "Very little skill exists to predict drought for a month or more in advance," Wilhite said.

Although decade-long droughts such as the Midwest experienced during the 1930s haven't recurred here of such long duration, they have occurred elsewhere in the world, according to KMTV meteorologist Carey Coleman. The drought in the Sudan in north-central Africa is extending into a whole generation. The southern United States has experienced drought in most of the last dozen years, and until two years ago the Western United States suffered under a severe drought that had lasted five or six years.

"Only so much precipitation falls worldwide at any given time, and to understand drought patterns it is helpful to take a hemispheric view," Coleman said. "Even if we have witnessed shorter drought cycles in recent years, the span of a human lifetime is much too short to infer much about our climate. Since the thunderstorms that produce rain come from the sun heating up moist air near the ground, once a drought sets in, it perpetuates itself because there is no ground moisture for the sun to heat up. It is hard to break the mode of droughts."

While technology has advanced to minimize the effects of droughts — such as the building of dams to store water, center-pivot irrigation systems, and pumps that tap into the aquifers — there are factors that offset those advances. An ever-increasing population, for example, brings heavier demand on whatever precipitation occurs. As an example, Oklahoma and Texas have so reduced the level of their aquifers through irrigation that now pumping water from the much deeper levels makes irrigating agricultural crops cost-ineffective. They have depleted a resource, Wilhite said. Many windbreaks built to control soil errosion in Nebraska have been destroyed so that center-pivot irrigation systems could be accommodated. Groundwater has become contaminated. And such industries as hydroelectric production and recreation, which didn't exist during earlier droughts, are water-dependent and place heavy burdens on resources.

"Cities are buying land for the water rights," Wilhite said. "Competition is creating a society that is becoming more and more vulnerable to water shortages."

As far as agricultural production is concerned, dryland farmers feel the

IAN DOREMUS/Lincoln Journal-Star

Droughts are not without their humor; this marker appeared on the muddy edge of Holmes Lake in Lincoln in June 1989.

effects of a lack of precipitation quickly, but they also recover quickly when it does rain. Farmers who depend on stored water for their crops may have supplies for a year or two or even three; stored water acts as a cushion to drought. But if the drought continues, it takes those irrigation-dependent farms much longer to recover because the groundwater aquifers, reservoirs, rivers and streams must refill.

Even though we have little ability to accurately predict droughts, farmers should evaluate the depth of their groundwater as well as predictions of high temperatures and low precipitation. When factors are considered high risk, farmers should make their decisions accordingly, Wilhite said. "They need to look at the probablilities. It's a gamble. Just planting a crop is not a small investment, and we all have to use water more efficiently."

We need to turn drought management into water management, Wilhite said.

DICK MEZZY/Lincoln Journal-Star

THUNDERSTORMS

"... the storm was close upon me, terrible to see and roaring. I cried more than ever now, for I was much afraid. The night was black about me and terrible with swift fire and the sending of great voices and the roaring of the hail."

— John G. Neihardt
Black Elk Speaks

A restless sky above the city in September 1967, brought many Lincolnites out to watch the seething clouds — until the storm broke and the heavenly ballet ended.

THUNDERSTORMS

Think of a thunderstorm as an automaton that creates itself of rain, hail, wind, lightning and thunder.

Thunderheads (cumulonimbus, officially) occur when the sun heats moist air near the ground. As the air warms, it rises to become white, puffy clouds. Nebraska's high surface temperatures provide a near-perfect environment for initiating those updrafts.

As the cloud grows in size, its upper surface meets cold air. As long as there are no strong winds blowing from the side, the thunderhead will keep growing — perhaps to more than 10 miles high. Drops of water move up and down inside this weather robot, forming bits of ice that can grow into large balls of hail.

It is as if when they recognize the monsters they have become, the thunderheads lose interest and self-destruct, dispensing 70 percent of the state's annual rainfall at the time it is most badly needed for crops. That's the good news. But when it falls in flood quantities, it brings the terror and the tears that John Neihardt refers to in *Black Elk Speaks.*

In Nebraska, thunderstorms typically occur 50 times a summer, usually in the late afternoon or early evening. A worldwide phenomenon, at any moment 1,800 storms are striking around the world, according to Ti Sanders in *Weather.*

Those who grow up in Nebraska are so accustomed to the puffy white clouds that become the ominous dark variety, forming quickly and dispensing their wealth, that they pay little attention. That complacency changes quickly when thunderstorms come close to home.

It happened to thousands of people on July 8, 1993, when winds of between 30 and 90 mph roared across the state. Never had Nebraska suffered such

TED KIRK/Lincoln Journal-Star

Axes thunked and chainsaws whined as Lincolnites cleaned up after severe winds raked the city in July 1993.

widespread tree damage. Trees were uprooted like radishes and broken apart like matchsticks. Roofs and porches took leave of the houses they were attached to that night, and falling trees brought down power lines. Between 10,000 and 15,000 homes and businesses were without power in Lincoln alone. Winds roared through the capital at 73 mph; in Kearney, at 90 mph.

The agricultural sector also took a serious hit in that storm. Farm damage was estimated at $100 million in southeast Nebraska alone, including $50 million in crop damage. The rest of the loss was in flattened grain bins and out-buildings and in center-pivot irrigation units, rolled up like great balls of metal knitting yarn.

Two weeks earlier, on June 24, "Powerful thunderstorms with winds clocked at 77 mph ripped through Grand Island, knocking over power lines, snapping trees and damaging homes (250 in Hall County) and businesses,"

The Associated Press reported. The wind brought down 200 utility poles in the Southern Nebraska Rural Public Power District.

But pick a year — any year. Excessive wind is as much at home on the Plains as the prairie grasses. From an April 29, 1989, Lincoln Star news story: "Lorin and Nancy Schmidt knew Thursday night's thunderstorm was a wild one but didn't know how wild until they awoke Friday morning to find that a 60-foot silo and hay barn had disappeared from their dairy farm southwest of Tecumseh."

Jan. 9, 1990: "The Nebraska State Patrol said wind gusting in excess of 60 mph blew a dust storm across western Nebraska, causing low visibility that was blamed for a 10-vehicle pileup on I-80 and a fatal crash near Big Springs." From that same Associated Press news story, Scottsbluff firefighter Lt. Monte Connolly said the 85 mph winds there "took the water from the hoses right down the road," instead of where they were directed, toward a house that was burning.

In 1991, the Soil Conservation Service reported the state had 91,440 acres of soil eroded by damaging winds.

And on Aug., 2, 1992, a downburst — a strong, straight-line wind out of a thunderstorm — descended on Geneva at more than 60 mph, toppling a carnival Ferris wheel, bringing down trees and, with them, more power lines.

"Straight-line winds are thunderstorm winds that are not associated with a tornado," said Carey Coleman, KMTV meteorolgist. "These winds are caused by rapidly descending air from a thunderstorm, caused by the sheer weight of rain-cooled air, which becomes heavier than the surrounding air and falls to the ground. Or they can be caused by a diversion of mid-level winds down to the ground."

A severe thunderstorm watch is issued by the National Weather Service when its center in Kansas City, Mo., identifies conditions capable of, and likely to produce, severe storms. That watch changes to a warning when hail of at least three-quarters of an inch in diameter is observed and/or winds reach or exceed 58 mph. Sometimes the warning is issued based on the probability of such conditions that are inferred from a radar echo, Coleman said.

The kind of downburst that hit Geneva was not even known in weather circles until 1974. Theodore Fujita, flying over West Virginia to survey the storm damage of the rash of tornadoes that struck at that time, noticed a starburst of tree damage. When he investigated the June 24, 1975, crash of an Eastern Airlines Boeing 727 at Kennedy Airport in New York, Fujita hypothesized that the plane had been hit by the same kind of windburst. His hypotheses proved true, and now special microburst detection radars are being installed at airports across the nation, according to *USA Today*

WEB RAY/Lincoln Journal-Star

Trees at Holmes Lake in Lincoln took a beating under 45 mph winds in March 1980.

Weatherbook.

"To create the constant panorama of changing skies, winds and temperatures, something has to set those air masses in motion. That something is air pressure — the force air exerts on everything it touches. Air pressure is important for three reasons — it creates the wind . . . the up and down movement of air in low- and high-pressure areas creates cloudy or clear skies. . . . Since the air's pressure at any one place rarely stays the same for long, the winds and weather are constantly changing," as reported in *USA Today Weatherbook.*

In pioneer days, it was the wind that gave the dreaded prairie fire its impetus to char everything in its path. And during the drought of the 1930s, it was wind that filled the sky with topsoil, turning noontime to darkness and creating the Dust Bowl.

Even when the prairie winds are not on a rampage, they get a bad rap from the unaccustomed. Ernie Pyle, a newspaper columnist of World War II fame, once wrote in his nationally syndicated column: "To me that summer wind in the Midwest is one of the most melancholy things in all of life. It comes from so far and blows so relentlessly. . . . It just keeps coming like the infinite flow of Old Man River. You could — and you do — wear out your lifetime on the dusty Plains with that wind of futility blowing in your face. And when you are worn out and gone, that wind — still saying nothing . . . — is still blowing across the prairies and will blow in the faces of the little men who follow you, forever."

But there is an updraft to wind and that benefit also has affected Nebraska, compensating to some degree for the wind that pillages.

Not everyone could live on the bank of a stream. Homesteads often were located far from a surface water supply and hauling water could become a full-time job. The discovery of the state's abundant ground water allowed water to be tapped from wells, and that life-sustaining water was lifted by the unceasing wind via the prairie monument — the windmill.

As destructive as wild winds on the loose are, more people are killed by lightning every year than by any weather condition other than flash floods.

About 100 lightning bolts strike the earth every second, according to Stephen Kramer in *Lightning*. During a June 21, 1989, storm in Lincoln, the National Weather Service said lightning struck the ground 100 times every 15 minutes. Lightning is a very large electrical spark caused by electrons moving suddenly. The zig-zag flash shows the path electrons follow as they blast their way forward. Lightning can flash sideways, but those that cause the damage are the electronic exchanges that flash between the clouds and ground.

Lightning travels at 270,000 mph and can reach temperatures of 54,000 degrees, according to Jonathan Kahl in *Weatherwise*. By comparison, the surface of the sun is about 11,000 degrees. A bolt is most often three or four miles long but only an inch or two wide.

In 1969, Mr. and Mrs. Henry Ruterbories of Plainview learned more than they wanted to about lightning's destructive power. Three of their sons, Mike, 18, Gary, 16 and Joel, 13, were working in a hayfield when a thunderstorm came up and it began to hail. The three took shelter under a haystack but all were killed when lightning struck the haystack.

News reports and historical accounts are filled with deaths of fishermen, farmers, golfers, gardeners and bikers who were unable to get to shelter before a lightning bolt struck them. Four golfers on the Indianhead Golf Course at Grand Island had a memorable experience in 1992 when they were all knocked to the ground by the same bolt.

Lightning bounces around indiscriminately and strikes landmarks like Chimney Rock, the Brownville Concert Hall and the Sharp Building in Lincoln. It knocks out electric systems, sets off alarm systems and provides the spark to ignite buildings and the prairie itself.

In 1985, lighting started a grass fire that burned thousands of acres in

DEAN TERRILL/Lincoln Journal-Star

The winds that can devastate also run the mills that have long kept the water pumping on Nebraska farms.

northwest Nebraska, with canyons funneling the roaring flames and forests providing the fuel to keep the fire racing. In July 1989, a fire that charred 48,500 acres at Fort Robinson and the surrounding area was caused by lightning.

And while such an incident might go unreported in other states, in Nebraska, where football is the state's second obsession (after its weather), for the first time in the University of Nebraska's 102-year history, on Sept. 7, 1991, a Cornhusker football game with Utah State was delayed until the threat of lightning had passed.

It is lightning that produces thunder. Lightning's incredible heat, Kramer writes, explodes the air around the channel outward. The resulting sound is thunder. While those "great voices," as Neihardt called them, sound terrifying, thunder is the only part of a thunderstorm that is always harmless.

Hail is generated within violent updrafts that carry supercooled water droplets and ice particles up and down through the thundercloud in repeated cycles of melting and freezing. Once the weight of a hailstone exceeds the force of an updraft, it falls to the earth.

Nebraska's hailstorm season usually begins in April, is most common in June and ends in September, and Great Plains farmers lose more than $100 million annually to hail damage. A storm on June 18, 1970, cut a swath four

Journal-Star Files

When lightning struck the Sharp Building in downtown Lincoln in October 1960, a stone broken loose high above crashed to the street, wrecking a drugstore marquee, a traffic signal and a passing car.

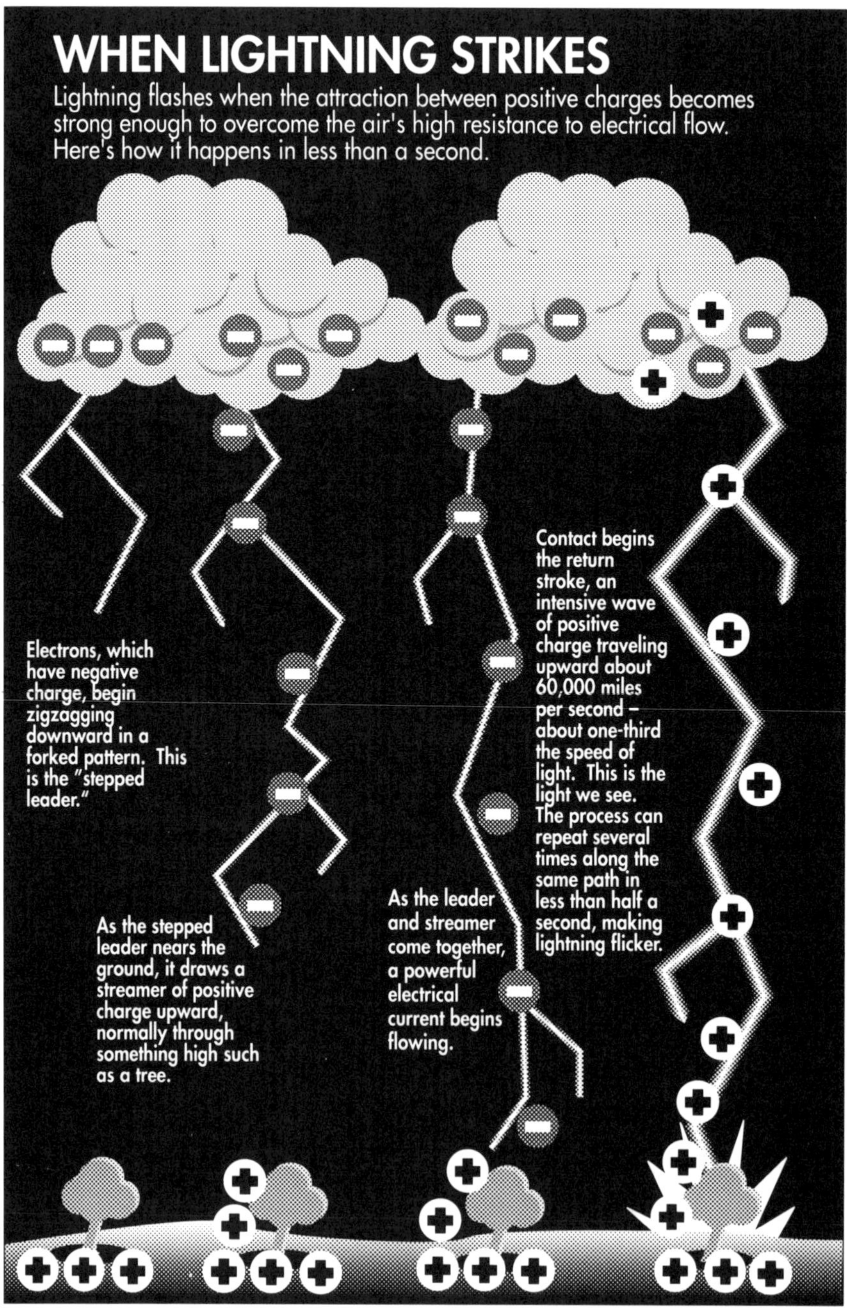
WHEN LIGHTNING STRIKES
Lightning flashes when the attraction between positive charges becomes strong enough to overcome the air's high resistance to electrical flow. Here's how it happens in less than a second.
Electrons, which have negative charge, begin zigzagging downward in a forked pattern. This is the "stepped leader."
As the stepped leader nears the ground, it draws a streamer of positive charge upward, normally through something high such as a tree.
As the leader and streamer come together, a powerful electrical current begins flowing.
Contact begins the return stroke, an intensive wave of positive charge traveling upward about 60,000 miles per second – about one-third the speed of light. This is the light we see. The process can repeat several times along the same path in less than half a second, making lightning flicker.

JAY BENSON/Lincoln Journal-Star

Lightning from a summer storm lights up the sky.

to eight miles wide through wheat and corn fields in southwestern Nebraska, causing a $5 million crop loss. In June 23, 1985, hail stripped some fields clean, including 32,000 acres in Saunders County alone. Insurance adjusters said it beat a 15-year record.

The Nebraska Panhandle lies in an area having the highest incidence of hail in the nation — Hail Alley, according to Merlin P. Lawson in *Climatic Atlas of Nebraska.* Reporters usually describe hailstone size in terms of marbles, golf balls or softballs. Perhaps a giant passed through Potter on July 16, 1928, and ordered a martini. In any case, the second largest hailstone ever documented by the National Weather Service fell that day — an ice cube suitable for a giant's cocktail. It was not until a thunderstorm struck Coffeyville, Kan., in 1971 that the 17-inch, 1½-pound Potter hailstone was outclassed. The Coffeyville cube measured 17½ inches.

"Only violently strong updraft winds can produce large hail," Coleman said. "It takes an updraft of at least 100 mph to produce a 3-inch-diameter hailstone and an updraft of at least 120 mph to produce a 4-inch stone. Large hail is an indication that a thunderstorm is strong enough to produce a tornado."

It would be nearly impossible to find a summer without serious hail damage somewhere in Nebraska, and this is just one example that can not be

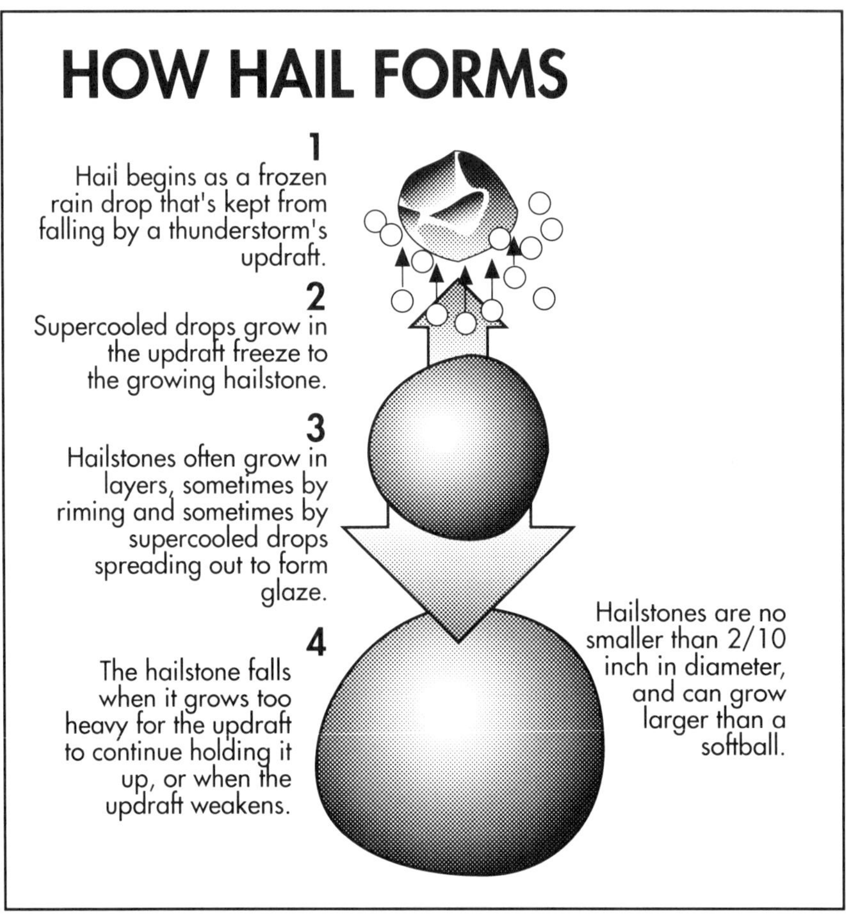

duplicated: On April 7, 1978, there were 9,000 windshields shattered by hail in Grand Island.

Hallie Meyers Nelson, who wrote *South of the Cottonwood Tree,* described a hailstorm of the mid-1930s: "He (her husband Jim) had hardly closed the door when the wind struck. It blew like a hurricane. Then we heard hailstones on the roof. They weren't ordinary hailstones — they were giant, jagged pieces of ice. Every minute was more frightening. The noise of the fierce wind and pounding hail was deafening. I saw a porch window pane shatter, then another. With a crash, the west kitchen window splintered as the huge stones ripped through the screen and struck the floor. . . . Every window on the north and west side of the house was shattered. Every screen, window shade, even the panel curtains were ripped to shreds. The floor was covered with hail, water and broken glass."

When Nelson looked outside, she saw that the brooder house that housed early broilers was gone. The chickens' bodies, beaten to death by hail, were scattered over the hillside. "This meat could be saved if we acted quickly. Their bodies were still warm and most of them bled (after their heads were cut off). We skinned instead of picked them. We scooped up hail from the drifts to pack them in until morning."

Wind, hail, lightning — fearful to all who understand the power of a thunderstorm. But one component has yet to be mentioned, and perhaps it is the most feared of all.

It is the tornado and deserves its own chapter.

Nebraska State Historical Society

TORNADOES

"Greenish clouds had whipped themselves into the shape of the bowl of a huge wineglass . . . a bowl that was twisted and blackened as though Appolyon and all the powers of darkness were to drink from it with wind for their wine. The stem of the tall glass touched the far horizon, poised there for a moment on the rim of the prairie and then, swaying dizzily, began moving across the open country."

— Bess Streeter Aldrich
The Rim of the Prairie

A twister photographed at Scribner in May 1902, lived up to its name, taking an interesting turn as it hovered over a Nebraska farmhouse.

TORNADOES

Nebraska has many strong weather systems. The jet stream is often passing between the state's southern and northern boundaries, flowing from west to east, and depending on its location, it allows arctic air to descend from the north or warm air to rise up from the Gulf Stream. It is the interaction of those two forces that produces most of the state's weather extremes. Add to that that the wind layer that crosses the Rocky Mountains is squashed as it comes in over the high altitudes. Then when it hits the Plains, that wind layer is pulled down to the lower elevation, causing great intensification, said KMTV meteorolgist Carey Coleman.

But the wind that makes headlines is the tornado.

"There are some winds that still baffle the scientist, and one of these is the most violent and terrifying wind of all. Though meteorolgists can explain and outline many of the conditions that produce it, no one has yet fully explained the mechanism of a tornado," Slater Brown wrote in *World of the Wind.*

Brown wrote those words in 1961, 19 years before the most baffling tornado in Nebraska history plowed through and around Grand Island on June 3, 1980, breaking all the known rules that tornadoes, at the top of their game, were supposed to play by.

While 87 percent of all tornadoes move from the southwest to the northeast, on that day of infamy, seven tornadoes swept into town from all different directions, leaving five dead and 200 injured. Ten years later, The Associated Press would name those tornadoes the "Story of the Decade."

T. Theodore Fujita has been an international expert on destruction since the end of World War II. With Nagasaki and Hiroshima both leveled by some "secret weapon" in the U.S. arsenal, it was he who determined only

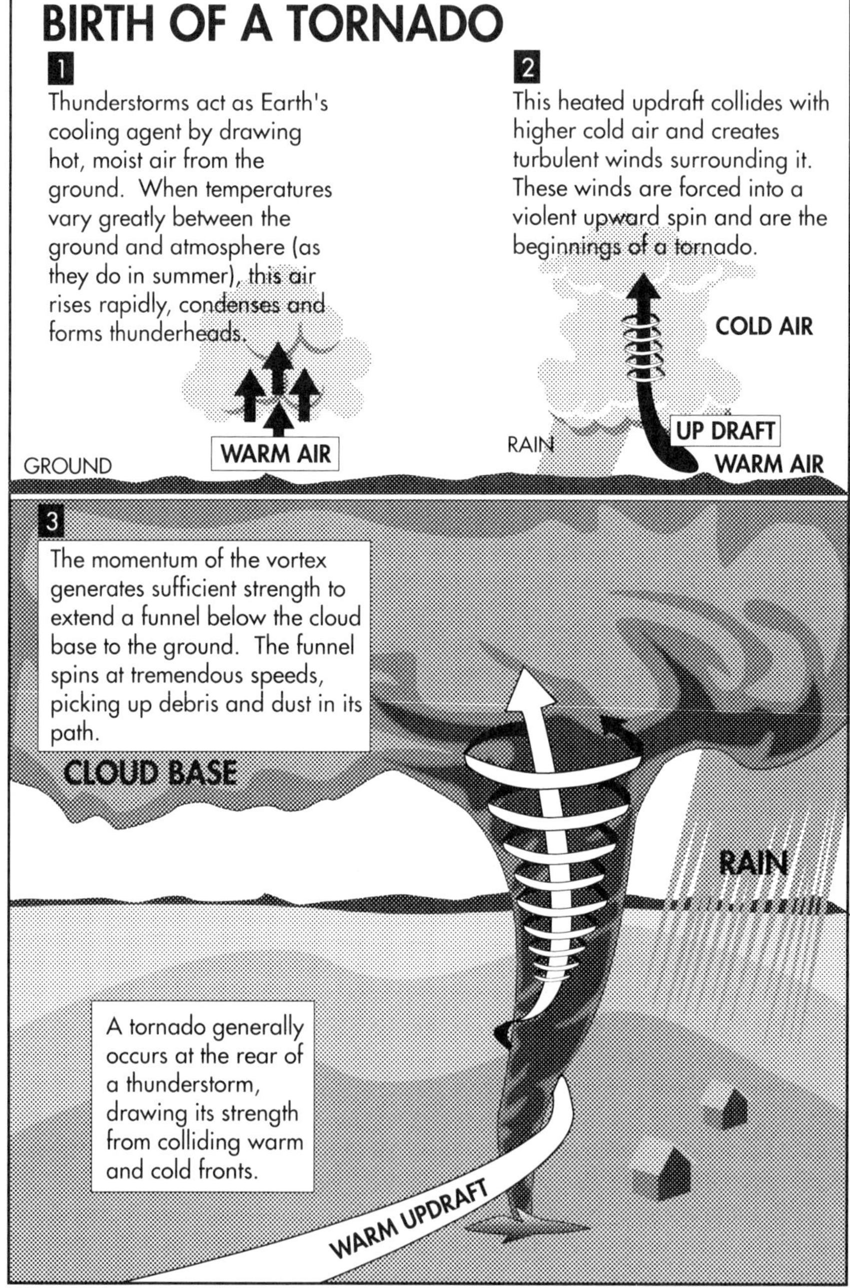
BIRTH OF A TORNADO
1
Thunderstorms act as Earth's cooling agent by drawing hot, moist air from the ground. When temperatures vary greatly between the ground and atmosphere (as they do in summer), this air rises rapidly, condenses and forms thunderheads.
WARM AIR
GROUND
2
This heated updraft collides with higher cold air and creates turbulent winds surrounding it. These winds are forced into a violent upward spin and are the beginnings of a tornado.
COLD AIR
UP DRAFT
RAIN
WARM AIR
3
The momentum of the vortex generates sufficient strength to extend a funnel below the cloud base to the ground. The funnel spins at tremendous speeds, picking up debris and dust in its path.
CLOUD BASE
RAIN
A tornado generally occurs at the rear of a thunderstorm, drawing its strength from colliding warm and cold fronts.
WARM UPDRAFT

Nebraska State Historical Society

One of Grand Island's 1980 tornadoes boils on the horizon.

two bombs had exploded by examining the shadowing effect they created. His Fujita, or F-scale, is still used to describe the intensity of tornadoes: F-0, winds up to 72 mph, light; F-1, winds from 73 to 112 mph, moderate; F-2, winds from 113 to 157 mph, considerable, F-3, winds from 158 to 206 mph, severe; F-4, winds from 207 to 260 mph, devastating; and winds above 261 mph, incredible.

Less than two percent of all tornadoes are in the "devastating" or "incredible" ranges.

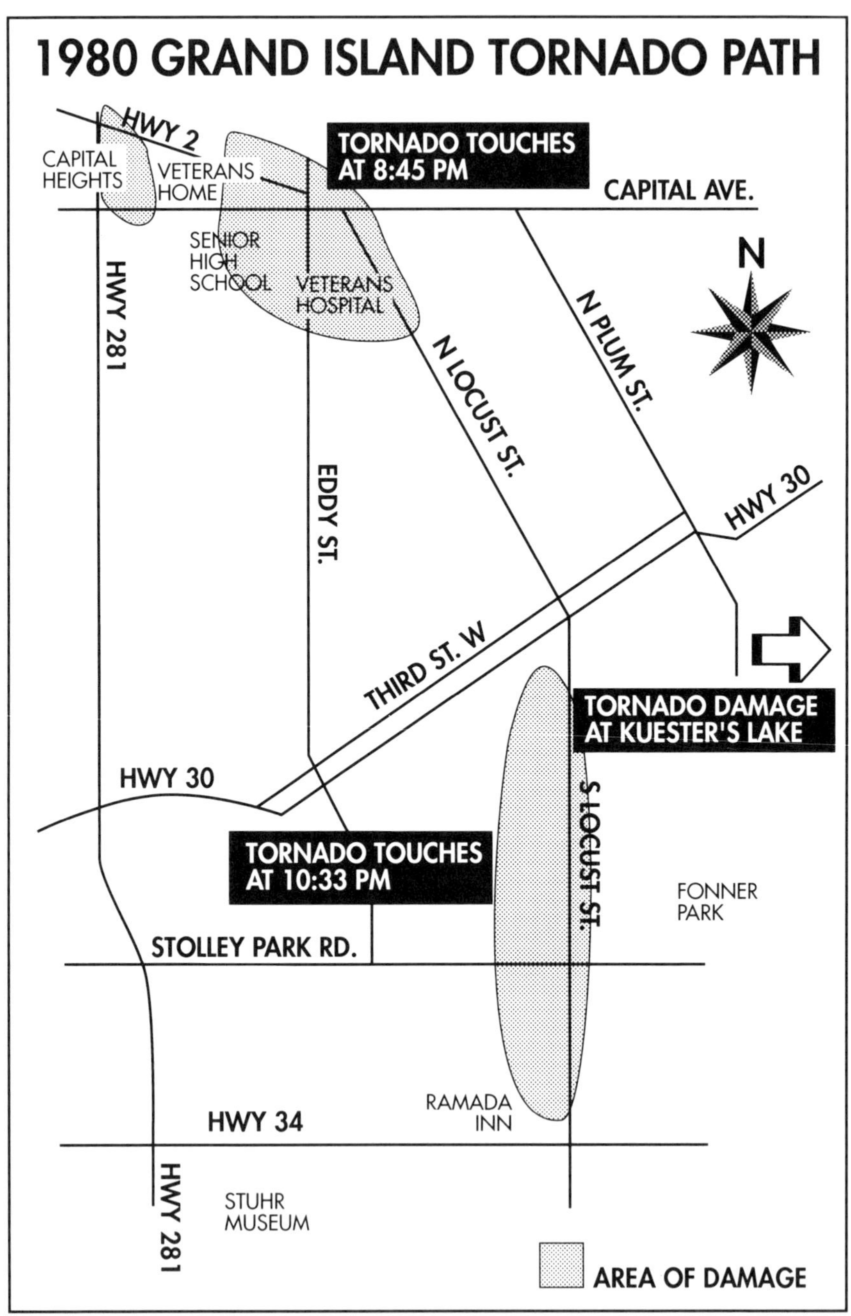
1980 GRAND ISLAND TORNADO PATH
HWY 2
CAPITAL HEIGHTS
VETERANS HOME
TORNADO TOUCHES AT 8:45 PM
CAPITAL AVE.
SENIOR HIGH SCHOOL
VETERANS HOSPITAL
N
HWY 281
N PLUM ST.
N LOCUST ST.
EDDY ST.
HWY 30
THIRD ST. W
TORNADO DAMAGE AT KUESTER'S LAKE
HWY 30
S LOCUST ST.
TORNADO TOUCHES AT 10:33 PM
FONNER PARK
STOLLEY PARK RD.
RAMADA INN
HWY 34
HWY 281
STUHR MUSEUM
AREA OF DAMAGE

Looking at the maps of the destruction in Grand Island, the international tornado expert could offer no explanation for the tornadoes' formation. From the maps of atmospheric conditions prior to the storms, Fujita said, "you wouldn't expect them to develop." He expressed surprise over the storms moving from the northwest to the southeast, instead of the typical southwest-to-northeast pattern.

Statistically, tornadoes strike quickly, traveling at about 40 to 50 mph, but apparently they liked Grand Island so well in 1980 they just came and stayed.

Dick Payne and his family watched one of the original funnels form over his farm home two miles west and four miles north of Grand Island. "The kids saw the buildings explode just to the north over there," he said. The family raced for the basement even as their home was being shredded.

"I've heard a lot about tornadoes, and people said they last only three to five seconds. Hell, this one shrieked and hummed around our house for 15 to 20 minutes," Payne was quoted as saying in a special edition of the Grand Island Independent. Meteorologist Don Davis said that in four hours the storm traveled only slightly more than 30 miles in an arc from Dannebrog to Phillips.

Tornadoes are supposed to turn left — counterclockwise — with an estimated wind speed of 200 to 250 mph, although some metereorolgists estimate the speed as much as three times higher. Two of the 1980 Grand Island tornadoes apparently made right-hand turns and another made a U-turn.

"Downed power lines looked like giant spider webs silhouetted against the illuminated sky. Debris made it hard to walk. Broken gas mains made it hard to breathe. People crying out for the missing made it hard to think," the Grand Island Independent reported.

Hall County Sheriff's Deputy Kelly Buck was at the intersection of U.S. 281 and Nebraska 2 and first saw the tornadoes when they were still in the sky north of the city. Before he knew it, one funnel was on top of him. With his emergency brake on and his foot jammed on the foot brake, his cruiser was dragged backward along the highway. The back window was sucked away, but he later drove away uninjured.

When they heard the roar at the Pagoda Lounge, the 15 or 16 people there crouched down around the piano bar and put their hands over their heads. They later pulled the body of Vietnam vet Ronnie Leece from the rubble. Danny Davenport tried to protect his fiance by covering her with his body under the canopy of a motel. He was hit on the back of the head with a beam and died later. There were three more deaths.

Volunteers searched for the missing all night. When morning came, the sight was overwhelming — 150 square blocks in Nebraska's third largest

HARALD DREIMANIS/Lincoln Journal-Star

Shocked Grand Island residents begin cleaning up after twisters destroyed 475 homes and apartments in 1980.

city had been flattened by the storm. There was at least $140 million in damage; 475 homes and apartment units were destroyed and 49 businesses razed. Additionally, 17 square miles of Hall County outside of Grand Island had felt the storm's wrath, and 55 farms in Hamilton County were damaged and two homes blown away.

Omahan Ben Nelson, who had been President Jimmy Carter's Nebraska campaign manager, urged the then-president to visit Grand Island. On his way back from Seattle a week later, Carter did make a brief stop. He said he'd visited the devastation of 21 tornadoes while he was governor of Georgia and "this is the worst I've seen."

The Grand Island tornadoes came out of a supercell thunderstorm, explained KMTV's Carey Coleman. While a routine thunderstorm has a life-span of about an hour, a supercell can produce severe weather for many hours. Once a supercell gets going, it creates its own environment, feeds on itself and tends to decrease other storm development in the area. The supercell-born tornadoes that struck Grand Island were pulling winds toward themselves from as far away as Kansas and Omaha. "This was an unusually fearsome storm," Coleman said. "It must have seemed like it would never end for the people of Grand Island."

"Tornadoes appear when warm, moist, tropical air from the gulf collides with cold, dry polar air from Canada," Slater Brown wrote. "The collision of this polar and tropical air is visible in the clouds, one group of clouds coming from the northwest, the other from the southwest. When they meet they form a dark green boiling mass. . . . They roll over each other in a well-developed whirl. . . . From this convulsion of clouds there emerges a spur or prong which, rapidly lengthening, gropes toward the Earth and sways to and fro like the elephantine trunk of some indistinguishable monster. As the trunk lengthens, the trumpeting of the wind begins. Then the lethal tip reaches downward, touches the Earth and the devastation has begun."

"The violent whirling action of the winds — inward and upward — is the main characteristic of a tornado," Frank W. Lane wrote in *The Violent Earth*. "Within the main funnels of large tornadoes are miniature twisters, or suction vortices, as Fujita calls them. Tornadoes reach deafening cre-

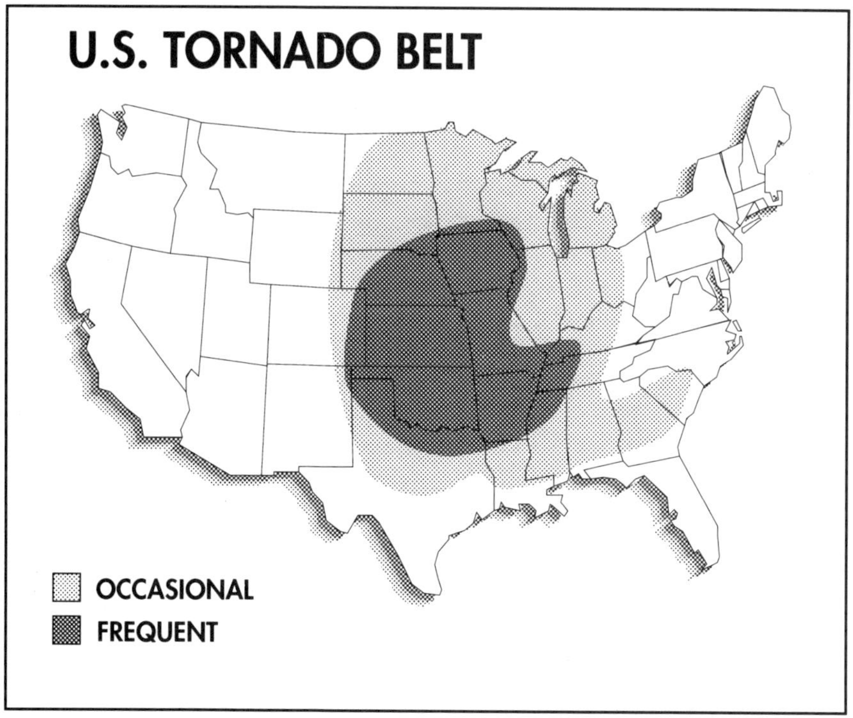

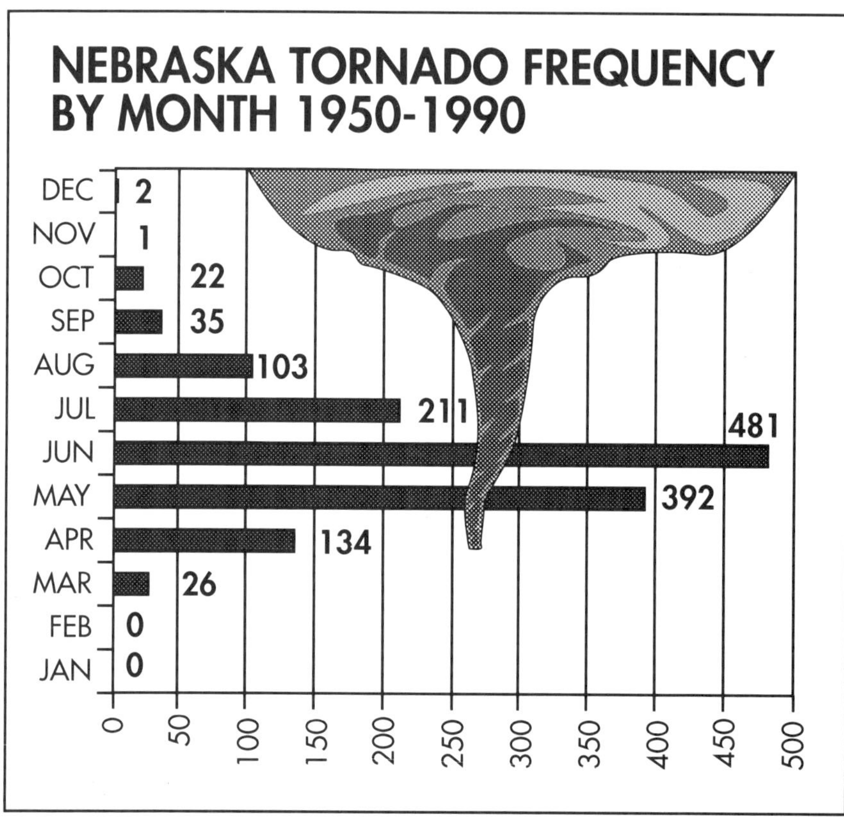

scendos when they strike — the bellowing of a million mad bulls, the roar of ten thousand freight trains or a million cannons, are common descriptions.

"Sand and gravel are whipped along with such force that they enter human bodies like shotgun pellets," Lane wrote.

Tornadoes are not always recognized as they approach because they sometimes come wrapped in dust or rain, Coleman said.

The notion that the incidence of tornadoes is on the increase in Nebraska is only due to better reporting. And the very common statement by awed viewers of tornadoes' devastation — "It's a wonder more people weren't killed" — is directly related to a better warning system that allows people to take cover, the National Weather Service says.

The most dangerous place to be when a tornado hits is a mobile home. In the United States tornadoes killed 304 people between 1985 and 1990. Of those, 99 people — nearly one third — were killed in mobile homes, according to *USA Today Weatherbook.*

A tornado watch is issued when either eyewitnesses see a tornado or fun-

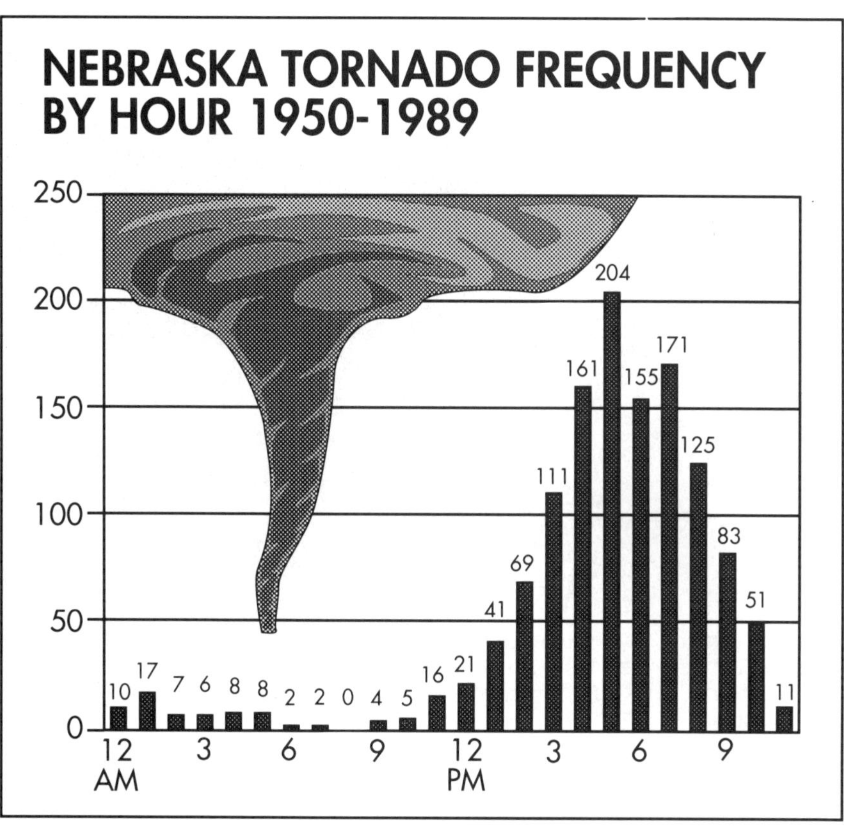

nel clouds or radar indicates the possibility, Coleman explained. A thunderstorm warning becomes a tornado watch when conditions are extremely unstable or there is enough shearing in the atmosphere for cloud rotation to begin that could lead to the spawning of tornadoes. The results of that cyclonic rotation are called funnel clouds until they reach the ground. Then they are tornadoes.

Commonly, tornado season begins in Nebraska on April 1. But nobody in south-central Nebraska has taken that seriously since March 13, 1990. The storm that snaked into the state that night spawned at least 10 separate tornadoes that played wipeout for 110 miles and raised havoc in 21 counties. One twister laid a track of devastation from east of Red Cloud to Sutton; the town of Lawrence was especially hard hit. In that town of 350 people, 68 buildings, including 53 residences, were damaged — some destroyed. Four businesses, including the grain elevator and lumber yard, were totally flattened. A piece was torn off of Lawrence High school, leading to water damage inside. Sutton was better off, with 20 homes and 14 businesses damaged.

Nebraska State Historical Society

A tornado that struck Omaha on Easter Sunday 1913, was described as "an enormous hollow cylinder, bright inside with lightning flashes, but black as blackest night all around."

York County had the most extensive damage of any county, with an almost $9 million loss.

"It (the tornado that hit the south edge of York) just reached around and took $250,000 out of my pocket," Jerry Bair, owner of Ag Flight, an uninsured crop-dusting service, told The Lincoln Star. A 49-car train west of Waco was tipped over as if it were a toy. Large flocks of migrating geese, downed by hail, littered a large area around Gresham.

Twelve rural power districts were damaged, including York County Rural Power District, where the loss was $312,000. The blackness of the night added to the fear.

The final tally was $4.7 million in losses to 550 homes and businesses, $5 million to public property and $81 million to agriculture.

Another March tornado made history when it struck Omaha on March 23, 1913.

On rare occasions, people have seen the inside of a funnel as it passed over their heads or nearby. One of those was Milton Tabor, editor of the Topeka Daily Capital, who was picnicking on Easter Sunday 1913. In his newspaper report he wrote: "It was an enormous hollow cylinder, bright

Journal-Star Files

Homeless Omahans took shelter where they could in the wake of the Easter Tornado.

Nebraska State Historical Society

Omaha's Sacred Heart Academy one of many casualties of the twister on March 23, 1913.

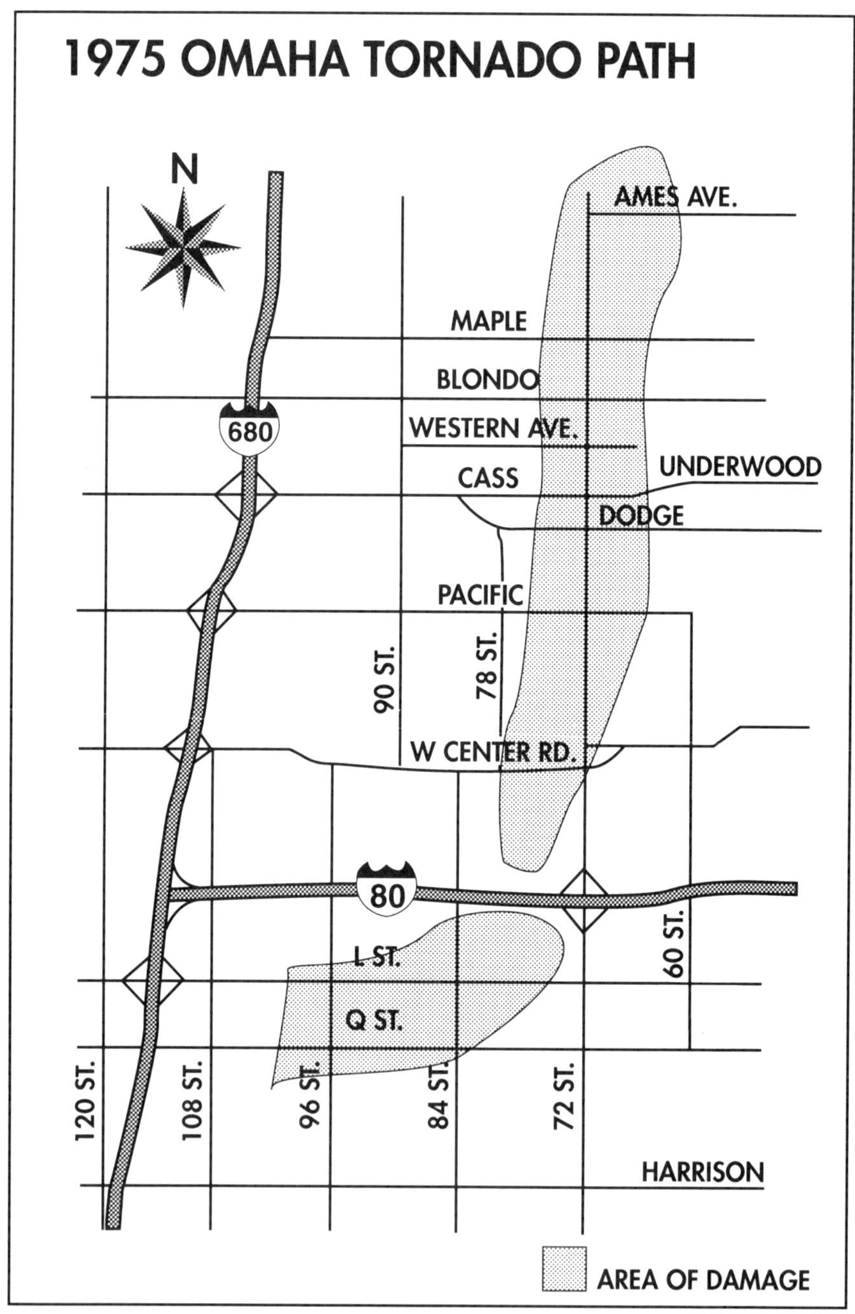
1975 OMAHA TORNADO PATH
N
680
AMES AVE.
MAPLE
BLONDO
WESTERN AVE.
UNDERWOOD
CASS
DODGE
PACIFIC
90 ST.
78 ST.
W CENTER RD.
80
60 ST.
L ST.
Q ST.
120 ST.
108 ST.
96 ST.
84 ST.
72 ST.
HARRISON
AREA OF DAMAGE

inside with lightning flashes, but black as blackest night all around. The noise was like 10 million bees, plus a roar that beggars description."

Tabor's sighting is significant because that same tornado touched down in Omaha later in the day, and in 12 minutes it took the lives of 140 people, injured 400 and destroyed 2,800 homes, according to the Omaha Daily News.

On that Easter Sunday, two tornadoes came in a northeasterly direction from the Greenwood area. The northbound twister did its greatest damage in Yutan, where 18 people died and the town was set afire. Less than an hour later, a second twister struck the Omaha suburbs of Florence, Dundee and Ralston. It skipped to 40th and Farnam streets, cutting a three-block path of destruction as it headed for the Missouri River and Council Bluffs.

At 24th and Lake in Omaha, 25 people were killed in the Idlewild Pool Hall; one lone survivor was dug from the wreckage 12 hours later. At that same intersection, 17 moviegoers were killed when the Diamond Theater was leveled. The Omaha World-Herald reported 50 fires broke out in the storm's aftermath.

The myth that any area is tornado proof is just that — only a myth. Some believe that tornadoes bypass downtown areas because something about the height of the buildings causes them to veer away. They cite as proof the fact that the two devastating tornadoes that struck Omaha both skirted the downtown area, but that is only because tornadoes strike a very small land area. The theory was blown away when a 30-story building in downtown Houston, Texas, took a direct hit from a tornado in November 1993, Coleman said.

The popular myth that tornadoes never strike the same place twice was proven untrue in Omaha on May 6, 1975.

"Roaring like an oncoming freight train, a string of tornadoes smashed into Omaha, killing at least three and possibly five and injuring more than 135. Both Gov. J.J. Exon and Mayor Edward Zorinsky called it the worst disaster they had seen," the Omaha World-Herald reported the next day.

"Patrolman David Campbell rode with the devil Tuesday evening over a six-mile route that left Omaha's once-glittering 72nd Street strip in mangled darkness," the paper reported. As he pulled out onto 72nd Street, the tornado was right beside him. "It was funny, white on the outside, I guess that was the rain, there was an awful lot of it . . . and black stuff in the middle, lumber and stuff," Campbell related. "It was awful at Pacific (Street). The air was filled, cars were sailing about, the (electrical) lines were flying. I thought I was going to be electrocuted. Everything lit up blue for a hundred feet around." Power poles were flying about and Campbell veered from side to side to avoid them, before the twister lifted and disappeared.

Leveled in the attack was the West Omaha Postal station, 800 S. 72nd St.; Baker's Supermarket, 72nd and Blondo streets; the Downtowner Motel,

Journal-Star Files

A tornado traces its path in the smashed homes and businesses left behind — as an Omaha twister did in 1975.

69th and Dodge streets; the Wentworth Apartment complex, 9525 U Plaza; and dozens of houses. Severely damaged were places like Nebraska Furniture Mart, 700 S. 72nd St., where a couple of dozen people took shelter in the store's bomb shelter; and Bergen-Mercy Hospital, 7500 Mercy Road.

Earlier that same year, on March 27, the city had a dress rehearsal for disaster when a tornado struck without warning, damaging 20 homes in southwest Omaha. It caused the staff at Bergen-Mercy to be on constant alert, the administrator said. With a 10- to 15-minute warning on May 6, patients were moved from rooms into corridors to avoid flying glass, 50 babies were removed from a nursery that could have been a death trap, and 40 patients were moved from a one-story self-care unit that was demolished by high winds.

A van was picked up on the south side of the hospital, carried over the roof and smashed down on the north side.

Omaha meteorologist Jim Zoller said the reason more people didn't die in the 10-mile path of destruction was because they took proper precautions.

Tornadoes happen all over the world, but nowhere as they do in Tornado Alley, which stretches from the Texas Gulf through the Dakotas.

The single worst year in the United States was 1992 with 1,302 tornadoes. The previous record year was 1987 with 912 twisters, but whether rising counts are due to better reporting or an actual increase in tornado activity is not perfectly clear. Most extensive in a two-day time period was in April 1974, when 148 tornadoes struck the eastern half of the United States, leaving 315 people dead and 6,142 injured, according ot Louis J. Battan in *Weather In Your Life.* Based on 1,000 random tornadoes, the average length of time for a twister to pass one location is 20 seconds. The total average life expectancy of a tornado is only eight minutes. They travel a little more than 13 miles at about 45 mph., according to Slater Brown, but anyone who has been up close and personal with one will say there are no average tornadoes.

Tornadoes do wild and crazy things: In the Grand Island storm on June 3, 1980, the home of Daryll Thavenent was destroyed but the refrigerator remained standing. Inside, with the door latched shut, was Daryll's wrist watch and two sets of keys. Everything was gone from the house except a jar of flowers on a kitchen counter. During a May 30, 1951, tornado in Scottsbluff, an egg was found with its shell uncracked but a neat hole through which a bean had been driven into the yolk. There are other egg tales, like crates being moved long distances without breaking a shell. And stories of chickens plucked clean of their feathers. Lane wrote that a two-ton station wagon was picked up, carried a fifth of a mile and thrown through the roof of a house.

All kinds of animals — horses, cows, hogs, sheep — have had the thrill of flight. Children and babies have sailed aloft and then been deposited unhurt but filthy from the debris that fills the tornado's vortex. Such was the case of a small boy at Stuart on July 9, 1884, who was picked up, blown a half-mile and set down unhurt. Houses sometimes are lifted like feathers. Brown told of Robert Reed of Irving, Kan., sweating out a tornado in his house. The twister lifted the house so gently that Reed opened his front door to step out to see what was going on and fell the 25 feet his house had risen in the air.

In *Conquering the Great American Desert,* Everett Dick wrote of a 1878 tornado that swept through Cherry County, leaving a deposit of slime, mud, rushes, fish and turtles. And there are many evidences of water having rushed up inclines across the prairie. On the Olof Hawkinson farm north of Minden, Hawkinson watched while his horse, hayrack and wagon flew

DAVE FAHLESON/Lincoln Journal-Star

In June 1984, this twister touched down south of Waverly.

away. He ran for the barn and in a short while the horse came walking in, unhurt except for a few wire cuts. Tornadoes are famed for driving straw through wooden planks and nails into boards — headfirst.

During the 1975 Omaha tornado, the only thing structural left standing above ground level at one residence was a porch rail. But not one dish in the portable dishwasher inside had even been cracked.

At about the time the tulips are all out of the ground, warm air begins moving into Nebraska from the south while cold arctic air still claims the upper levels. When they begin to vie for superior position, the turmoil becomes ugly. Sirens sound, hearts beat faster, fear restricts the heart area and Nebraskans think seriously about relocating.

And for good reason.

■ McPherson County, May 22, 1933: "A south wind that started as a breeze at sunup in the Sandhills grew stronger as the day wore on. By noon it was a howling wind, carrying clouds of red dust that hid the sun," according to the North Platte Telegraph. "Before that terrifying afternoon was over, McPherson's first and only tornado had ripped across the hills just northeast of Tryon, dealing death and destruction to a half a dozen farms. At the Pyzer place, six people, three of them children, were killed. The McIntyre sisters died in the destruction of their home a little farther on. At the Waits farm, the house and all its contents were carried away leaving Mr. Waits and other members of the family badly injured."

■ Hebron, May 9, 1953: "This huge black cloud out of the southwest with that black tail of disaster descending upon us, and Hebron stood powerless, defenseless, directly in its path. Then with the roar of an express train it entered our town, ripping, howling, screaming and destroying everything in its path," a Hebron resident wrote. That black tail of disaster took five lives, injured 69, destroyed 24 homes, Hebron High School, and 35 businesses. Many more buildings were damaged. Forty-one years earlier Hebron High School, at the same spot, had been flattened by a tornado that also did considerable damage to the town — speaking the final word on whether or not tornadoes strike the same place more than once.

■ Milford, April 25, 1957: The myth that Milford's location in relationship to the confluence of the Blue River and Wild Plum Creek made it tornado-proof was totally blown apart when the Seward County town of 980 took a $1.5 million hit in 1957. Paul Cast, who lived on a farm southwest of town, was killed and 20 people were hospitalized with storm injuries. Forty-nine houses, eight businesses and 14 farms in the area were totally destroyed, leaving 200 homeless.

■ Wolbach, St. Edward, Tilden, Benedict, Bradshaw, May 5, 1964: State Climatologist R.E. Myers wrote about the tornadoes' path in rural areas, outside the five towns: "The destruction was total for the 70 miles in the di-

Journal-Star Files

A Bradshaw farmer surveys some of the damage done by a tornado that cut a swath 70 miles long through central Nebraska in May 1964.

rect path of the tornado. All buildings, machinery, automobiles, fences, power lines were completely destroyed. It was as if an enormous vacuum cleaner had swept the path clean of vegetation, loose dirt and all other movable objects.

"Few recognized it as a tornado until it was close enough to see that the cloud was churning and full of debris. . . . One farmer said that he watched the cloud approaching from the kitchen window. He followed its progress over a mile, under the impression that it was heavy rain or hail, and did not recogonize it as a tornado until it entered his barnyard and he saw debris, machinery and livestock whirling in the cloud. The family was just clearing the basement steps when the house was carried away."

Four deaths and approximately 50 injuries resulted from that tornado. It is remarkable that the loss of life was not greater in view of the total destruction of 74 homes and major damage to 36 more, Myers wrote.

■ Primrose, May 8, 1965: Only the school and 14 houses were left standing after a killer tornado roared through Primrose. Four people died and 46 homes were destroyed; one street in the two-street town of 117 was totally demolished. The wind's power was demonstrated in the 18 railroad cars — each loaded with seven tons of gravel — that were tipped over like playthings.

■ Arcadia, April 20, 1974: The business community of the town of 410 was left in ruins, with 13 buildings damaged, including three that were leveled along with Sacred Heart Catholic Church. Twenty-one years earlier a tornado had struck a farm near Arcadia, killing 10 people at a family gathering.

■ Madison, June 16, 1990: The Madison County seat was still struggling to recover from recent flooding of Taylor and Union creeks when a tornado struck at 7 p.m., taking off a couple of roofs and bringing down dozens of trees. One house under construction had the appearance of a spilled box of Tinker Toys.

■ Minatare, June 9, 1991: A tornado slammed into the northwestern edge of town, destroying 19 homes and damaging 41 others, then skipped across six northeast Nebraska counties.

■ North-central Nebraska, June 15, 1992: Fourteen tornadoes touched down in a line from Otoe and Nemaha counties to Boyd County. Ten were sighted the next night and straight-line winds were confirmed at 80 mph. The storm front, which was 400 miles long, swept across eastern Nebraska, damaging 24 farmsteads in Seward County alone. Some were totally wiped out.

The list of the damage that Nebraskans have sustained from tornadoes would make an outsider wonder what, if anything, was left of the state. But the area is geographically huge, the touchdowns most often are both short in duration and distance, and as Everett Dick philosophically wrote, "The probability of a tornado striking a given place in Nebraska is small."

Besides, he wrote, "Although tornadoes are highly dramatic, winter storms presented much greater problems to early Nebraskans."

WEB RAY/Lincoln Journal-Star

BLIZZARDS

"The blizzard of the Plains was and is particularly dangerous for the tenderfoot, the newcomer, because it is often preceded by days and perhaps immediate hours of such benign calm; such deceptive warmth and sweetness of air."

Mari Sandoz
Love Song to the Plains

Utility poles and power lines in the David City area took a beating from a blizzard that roared across Nebraska in March 1966.

BLIZZARDS

While the Blizzard of 1888 held the crown for King of the Storms for 61 years, when the snow gods got angry in 1949, the blizzard of that year took the throne.

In 1949, it was Lincoln weatherman R.A. Dyke who broke the historic bubble of the Blizzard Club of 1888 when he spoke at the club's annual meeting. It was there that he said, "Jan. 3-5, 1949, was the worst blizzard that ever visited Nebraska." His speech came a week later than it had been scheduled; the blizzard of 1949 had forced a delay in the earlier blizzard's annual observance.

Marilyn Keenan Maxson of Ord could never be convinced that there ever had been a worse blizzard than the one in 1949. Her surgical scar has disappeared but her memories of the fear, pain and unimaginable cold will never fade. Now in her mid-50s, she said, "I still panic every time a snowstorm starts."

She was 12 years old in 1949 and lived with her parents, Everett and Lena Keenan, and a sister on a farm about 10 miles east of Ericson in Wheeler County. The family had been snowed in there since the 1948 Thanksgiving Day storm. "We'd plow the roads open, but they'd drift shut before we could get out," she said. It was after the January blizzard struck that Marilyn got an ache in her side that would not subside.

Her parents finally decided she had appendicitis, a potentially mortal situation, with no way off that isolated farm and all telephone lines down. As her condition worsened, her parents decided to try to get her to the hospital at Burwell, 47 miles away. They knew a neighbor who lived a mile and a half away and had a car stalled on U.S. 281, a mile farther on. They made Marilyn a bed in a lumber wagon, covered her with blankets and started out at 8 a.m. With the team pawing through drifts all the way, it was noon by the time they arrived at that neighboring farm. Marilyn's sister remained there, but it took another two hours for Marilyn and her parents to get to the stalled car on which their hopes depended. When they reached it on the highway at about 3 p.m., nothing could get the car's engine to turn over.

When a gasoline tanker came by, the three joined the driver in the truck's cab. But a few miles on, a stalled car on the highway blocked their route. Everett knew the Dunning Ranch was only half a mile away and set out on foot, hoping to find the keys there that might move the stalled car. As he left the truck, he told the driver, his wife and child that if he didn't come back, they were not to try to survive in the truck but that they, too, should get out and walk to the Dunning Ranch. "I never thought I'd see him again," Marilyn said.

Everett came back with a log chain over his shoulders and his face totally frost covered. Attempts to move the stalled car failed and the four finally walked to the Dunning Ranch, a hike that resulted in Lena's legs freezing. They spent the night there. "The next day my dad walked 12 miles on top of drifts to get to a telephone to call for help. My dad was a true hero," Maxson said.

A Spalding ham radio operator heard Everett's SOS and put out a plea for a plane at the Dunning Ranch, where a circle with a cross in its center had been stomped out in the snow. Not one, but two small planes arrived. Everett would not let Marilyn go with the first pilot because, "He didn't like the dangerous way he landed," Marilyn said. She went to the Ord Hospital with the second pilot, Don Durrey, who landed with skis on his plane. "I was scared and I cried. I had never flown before." Her dad and the first pilot followed the mercy flight to Ord, where Marilyn was operated on yet that day.

The next day, a snowplow came past the Dunning Ranch with a bread truck in its wake, headed for St. Paul. Lena Keenan caught a ride with that truck to the hospital in St. Paul to have her frozen legs treated — legs that gave her trouble the rest of her life, Maxson said.

It was at least 10 days before that first neighbor, where Marilyn's sister had stayed, learned whether the rest of the family had survived.

When Nebraska historian A.E. Sheldon published *History and Stories of Nebraska* in 1926, he identified the state's great blizzards as Dec. 1, 1856; April 13, 1873; and Jan. 12, 1888.

But had he lived to update his history in 1994, accuracy would have demanded 1949 and 1975 be added.

At the very least.

While hardly a winter can be identified during Nebraska's history when there were no snowstorms to cause people to press their noses to windows

Journal-Star Files

One casualty of the blizzard that struck Harlan County in March 1912, was a westbound Burlington train that became stuck east of Republican City. A rescue engine was sent from from Red Cloud, 40 miles east, to back the coaches — including a dining car — into Naponee.

to watch the spectacle — storms that made the front pages of newspapers — a blizzard is something different.

To qualify, it needs three components: the presence of snow — either falling or on the ground or both — raging wind, and temperatures that make thermometers gasp and shudder. In *Climatic Atlas of Nebraska,* Merlin P. Lawson says a blizzard is under way when winds reach 35 mph and temperatures drop to 20 degrees or lower. Historical accounts of blizzards are not always entirely accurate because of the vast geographical

Journal-Star Files

Frequent victims of Nebraska's fickle winter weather, this Burlington passenger train was stranded for 38 hours near Thedford in March 1913.

area of the state and the fact that outrageous weather is sometimes localized.

As examples, it snowed 24 inches in 24 hours at Hickman on Feb. 11, 1965. Kimball had the greatest snowfall in one season, 1958-59, with a record 105-inch total, according to David Ludlum's *American Weather Book.* The coldest Nebraska temperature ever recorded was at Camp Clark on Feb. 12, 1899, at -47. And Lincoln's coldest temperature, -33, was recorded on Jan. 12, 1974.

Nebraska winters are filled with various kinds of phenomena. Thundersnow is the same thing as the summer variety — but colder. Water vapor attracted to microscopic particles in the air becomes snow crystals. Depending on the temperatures, those crystals come in seven varieties — thin plates at the high of around 32 degrees to needles, hollow columns, sector plates, dendrites, sector plates and hollow columns again at about -8 degrees. Sleet forms when snow melts in a narrow area of warm air that is lying over a relatively cold air mass; when it refreezes, it becomes ice pellets or sleet. Freezing rain is snow that melts and falls into a shallow layer of cold air (below 32 degrees) lying at the surface and refreezes on contact with objects at ground level. Snow grains are partially melted and then re-

Journal-Star Files

Snow had drifted 30 feet deep on an Ainsworth farm by January 1962, forcing Red Cross workers to tunnel down to a water pump.

Journal-Star Files

Snow was plowed as high as the roofs of cars in the western Nebraska town of Gordon in the wake of the 1949 blizzard.

Journal-Star Files

Air Force helicopters based at Fort Riley, Kan., refueled at Lincoln before continuing on their rescue mission to central Nebraska as part of 1949's Operation Snowbound.

frozen snowflakes.

A storm track will determine the storm's components as well as the amount of snowfall. The greatest amount of snow is typically just to the north and east of the storm track. A change in the course of that track makes all the difference in what is delivered, Coleman said.

It is difficult to compare one blizzard's impact to others because of technological changes that evolve between them: central heating instead of wood or coal fires, indoor plumbing instead of wells and outhouses, mammoth road-clearing equipment instead of just waiting for the sun to clear a trail, sturdier buildings that provide more dependable shelter, and perhaps most importantly of all, the advent of electronic weather reporting and communications systems that wring some of the surprise out of the devastation. They all change the amount of discomfort a blizzard brings.

During the blizzard of 1949, Operation Snowbound with snow-blowers, tracked vehicles and transport as well as private planes, all drastically changed the survival odds with the relief efforts of food, medicine, hay for cattle and even a doctor who specialized in delivering babies.

The blizzard of 1949 began its march from the south — Oklahoma and Kansas — with winds hitting 65 mph. It revolved counter-clockwise, with

Journal-Star Files

Operation Snowbound bulldozers plowed wild patterns on the Nebraska prairie in 1949 as they fought to reach the thousands of people and millions of head of cattle marooned by the January blizzard.

sodden rain on its lower side. On its leading edge, chilled by incoming arctic air, the storm brought snow that a howling wind churned to blot out visibility. In Chadron, the snowfall was a record-setting 41 inches in 48 hours; the total for the month was 59.6 inches.

In April of that year, the Lincoln Sunday Journal and Star published a special edition about the Blizzard of 1949. It had taken almost that long for the state to recover.

That winter of 1948-49 brought a triple-header. Nebraskans had been punched severely by winter storms on Thanksgiving and again at Christmas in 1948, and some locations had not entirely dug out from under those storms. "We went under in November and didn't get out till March," a Holt County farmer said.

Journal-Star Files

Cattle weren't the only livestock endangered during the winter of 1948-49. A hole cut just under the eaves of this chicken house allowed farmers to feed and water their birds — although they had to dig the hatch clear of drifting snow every day.

The blizzard arrived the evening of Jan. 2, with falling temperatures and roaring winds. Snowfall measured at 30 inches was not uncommon. Snowdrifts were 50 feet deep in places — by meteorologists' measurements. It rained in the eastern part of the state and ice-skaters took to the streets in Lincoln.

The official Blizzard of 1949 (Jan. 2-3) ended 48 hours after it began, and reports of storm deaths started pouring in: elderly Harriet Brown, found frozen in her house at Gordon; Claude Hannibal of Alliance, who walked away from a stalled truck; Harmon Holleman, also of Gordon, found frozen in a haystack where he took refuge after his gasoline tanker stalled. "Scores of thousands of Nebraskans were trapped in their homes without food, fuel or medicine. Families sacrificed their furniture to feed kitchen stoves as snow piled as high as second-story windows," Dean Pohlenz wrote in the Journal and Star special edition.

Seventy-six people died in Nebraska — 571 in the total affected states. Nobody counted the toes and fingers, arms and legs that were lost to frostbite and freeze.

The storms of 1949 kept flexing their muscles and covered one-third of the United States. President S Harry Truman ordered the mobilization of Operation Snowbound, naming Lt. Gen. Lewis A. Pick, division engineer for the U.S. Army Corps of Engineers stationed in Omaha, to head the project.

It was Pick who formulated the plan for development of the Missouri River Basin that was put into effect as the Pick-Sloan plan — a plan that continues to figure in Nebraska's flood control. He had been appointed chief of engineers for the Army on March 1, 1949.

For blizzard relief efforts, Pick set up headquarters in Alliance. The Omaha headquarters of the Fifth Army had 296 pieces of snow equipment ready for action, and other military units were called to become part of Operation Snowbound. The Tenth Air Force used C-47s and D-C3s to drop tons of hay to starving lifestock. The Nebraska National Guard joined the effort, and in Nebraska 79,500 snowbound people were freed, nearly 34,000 miles of roads were opened and 1.7 million head of livestock were liberated.

The post-World War II baby boom was at full throttle that winter of 1948-49, and Dr. David Ikast, flight surgeon with the National Guard in Lincoln, was flown into Pierce where he delivered 17 babies in 20 days.

Private pilots in everything from puddle jumpers to crop-dusting planes delivered food, medicine and fuel. John Huff and Bill O'Brian were the first casualties of the air effort when the plane they were flying was so low it hit a power line and crashed into a farmhouse near Alliance, killing both men and leaving the plane's engine on the dining room table.

Livestock losses were estimated at 65,000 head of cattle, 45,000 sheep and 5,000 hogs. Near Ashby, a herd of 150 cattle driven before the wind wan

Journal-Star Files

Snowdrifts nearly engulfed a Burlington snowplow — helped along by two retired steam locomotives — as it labored to clear the railroad tracks near Alliance in 1949.

dered out on the glassy surface of a lake where they slipped and fell and were unable to rise, freezing to death.

The bad winter produced its lighter moments, too. The Bob Soefter family near Crawford had been snowbound from Dec. 31 to Feb. 5, but their laying hens kept on doing what hens do best. When a bulldozer crew broke through the drifts, every basket and container on the place was filled with eggs, as well as an 86-dozen overflow on the kitchen floor.

The power of drifted snow is best demonstrated by its ability to bring mighty railroad engines to a whimpering halt, an experience that happened on every line that served the state. At that time, trains still were the preferred mode of transportation for both passengers and freight.

On the Burlington line between Hyannis and Alliance, men and machines labored in zero-degree temperatures for 96 hours to free two engines, a snowplow and a coal car. In an attempt to clear the line, the plow was rammed forward by the two train engines. Not only did the engines wheeze to a stop, but the 40-foot walls of the drift came down, burying the entire train. The engineers and firemen were freed by frantic shovelers, but as the engines cooled, the melting snow froze. Forty-eight hours later the rear engine was freed from its snowy prison, a solid block of ice. Four days after the start of the effort, the line was finally opened by men working around the clock.

A trainman was killed on Jan. 18 when a doubleheader on the Union Pacific rammed a huge drift near Stapleton. The plow caromed off the icy face of the drift, buckled back and sheared off the sides of two locomotives.

The Chicago & North Western fought in vain to keep its tracks open in northern Nebraska. W.L. Mueller, a division superintendent who had been railroading for 35 years, said of other winters, "They were all toys compared with this one."

The Union Pacific used 14,000 employees to crew 15 railroad rotary plows, 33 railroad wedge plows, 124 flame throwers and 180 bulldozers in its attempt to keep its stock rolling.

Newspaper accounts estimated 7,500 passengers were stranded on as many as 50 stalled trains between Illinois and Idaho.

Both Life and Time magazines sent reporters and photographers to tell the blizzard story to the nation. The Time reporter called the snowbound area "a great white ruin."

Even though that early January blizzard was officially over, severe snowstorms kept dumping on the state with deadly regularity. When a school bus stalled on Jan. 19 near Gordon, the teacher led her 13 students to the nearby Gordon Creek Hereford Ranch, where they were not dug out until Feb. 12. With a captive student body, teacher Celia Sandoz taught classes every day.

The winter of 1949 was stubborn in its refusal to go away. On Feb. 6, another series of storms that would plague snow fighters for more than a month struck. It was Feb. 26, when Pick declared Operation Snowbound successful. But 10 days after the official arrival of spring, winds piled up fresh drifts across the Nebraska Plains, Pohlenz wrote. "Hays Center was completely cut off when winds whipped a 23-inch snowfall into towering drifts on March 30. Broken Bow had 12 inches; Burwell, 10; North Platte, 15, where schools were closed."

But no blizzard has been memorialized like the blizzard of 1888. In addition to the club formed by people who had survived that storm, at least one song was published nationally and millions of words have been written. It was called "The School Children's Blizzard" because it struck at just about the time school was being dismissed for the day. Many of the resulting

Nebraska State Historical Society

One heroine of the 1888 blizzard — also called "The School Children's Blizzard" — was teacher Minnie Freeman (left), who tied her young charges together in single file and led them to safety from their sodhouse school at Mira Valley.

deaths were those of children, and many of the heroines were teachers.

It was a letter to the editor published in the Lincoln Sunday Journal and Star in early January 1940 that gave birth to the "January 12, 1888 Blizzard Club." The letter, written by Mrs. H.J. Kierstead of Lincoln, told of the experiences of her grandparents during that storm. During a recess of the Nebraska Unicameral, Mrs. Kierstead's letter was discussed by legislators with plans to observe the anniversary. Survivors met for dinner at the Lindell Hotel on Jan. 12, 1940. The club's objective was to collect the stories and to publish a book of reminiscenses. "The boys and girls of 1888 have undertaken this task, believing that the more their descendents know about what it cost the pioneers to transform the blizzard-swept prairies into many great states, the better fitted they will be to carry on the work so well begun by their parents and grandparents," John Brady wrote about the blizzard club's book, *In All Its Fury.*

It was the United States Army Signal Service that recorded the weather at the end of the 19th century. Reviewing those records of January 1888 caused Lincoln weatherman Ray A. Dyke to write: "The blizzard of 1888 was notable not simply because of the low temperatures, for other cold waves have been colder. Neither was the snowfall remarkably heavy, nor the depth on the ground as compared with many other occasions. It was the combination of the three factors, namely the gale winds, the blinding snow, and the extremely rapid drop in temperature from winter comfort level to well below zero, which together made the blizzard most dangerous."

The temperature at Valentine, 30 degrees above zero on the morning of Jan. 12, dropped 36 degrees in eight hours and finally bottomed out at -35. At Crete, the cold wave signal was hoisted at 1:30 p.m. Who paid attention? The temperature was between 25 and 30 degrees above zero. But by 4:10 p.m., the wind had come to life, shifting from the southwest to the northwest, and the temperature fell 18 degrees in less than three minutes! In Lincoln, snowfall was measured at 7 inches, but the snow in the air that was piling up inside houses that had the slightest crack in door or window, or driven right through clothing, was not only falling snow but was being swept up off the ground. Wind velocities between 40 and 60 mph were common.

"The morning of Jan. 12 was calm and warm. School children played outside in shirt sleeves. Then, literally without warning, the storm roared down from Canada at 50 mph. Temperatures dropped 36 degrees. Snow up to 8 inches covered the Great Plains. Furious winds swirled the snow into a blinding, life-threatening blizzard," wrote Lincoln historian James L. McKee.

"More than 1,000 people died. (One hundred of them in Nebraska. Twenty died in Holt County alone.)

"This was the Blizzard of '88, the storm that covered nearly one-third of the nation," McKee wrote.

"Three young women school-teachers became famous as Nebraska heroines of this storm," Sheldon wrote. They were Louise Royce of Plainview; Etta Shattuck of Inman; and Minnie Freeman of Mira Valley.

"Miss Royce started from her schoolhouse with three children to go to a house only a few yards distant. They lost their way and the children were frozen to death. Miss Royce, after being out all night, was rescued the next day so badly frozen that one of her limbs was taken off.

"Miss Shattuck sent her children safely home at the first signs of the storm, but lost her own way and wandered to a haystack. She crept into the hay and lay there three days before she was discovered by a farmer, coming to get hay for his stock. Two of her limbs were frozen and had to be taken off. She was removed to her home at Seward, where she died a few weeks later.

"Miss Freeman tied her children together in single file with herself at the head of the line, and thus guided them through the storm to the nearest farmhouse where all were sheltered.

TED KIRK/Lincoln Journal-Star

Bolts of lightning dance over Nebraska's Capital City during a late fall storm in 1993.

GERIK PARMELE/Lincoln Journal-Star

RANDY HAMPTON/Lincoln Journal-Star

ABOVE: Drought conditions across Nebraska took their toll on the state's corn crop in the summer of 1991. LEFT: Straight-line winds raked Lincoln in July 1993, leaving tumbled fences, damaged roofs and fallen trees in their wake. Tree damage was especially heavy in the older sections of the city, where specimens more than 50 years old were snapped off at the ground or uprooted completely.

TED KIRK/Lincoln Journal-Star

ABOVE: In the typical fashion of tornadoes that strike at random across Nebraska each spring and summer, the twister that hit Lawrence in March 1990, left some homes nearly intact, heavily damaged others and completely destroyed still more. RIGHT: This tree on a farm south of Milford was stripped of its leaves and left a broken skeleton by a tornado that struck in June 1992.

Journal-Star Files

ROBERT BECKER/Lincoln Journal-Star

Only a blasted foundation and mangled appliances remained after a tornado struck this rural Palmyra home in April 1991. The building was lifted clear and deposited in a field yards away (upper right in photo).

ROBERT BECKER/Lincoln Journal-Star

A tornado that struck near Garland in June 1992, left this tractor a twisted wreck, ripped the roof off the farmhouse and stripped trees of their leaves and branches.

TED KIRK/Lincoln Journal-Star

ABOVE: As the long, snowy winter of 1992-93 was ending, eastern Nebraska had to deal with the normally placid Platte River swelling over its banks and flooding surrounding farmland. RIGHT: Thomas Lake southwest of Omaha broke through its dike in mid-March, undercutting a highway and sending floodwaters swirling over the countryside.

TED KIRK/Lincoln Journal-Star

IAN DOREMUS/Lincoln Journal-Star

Employees and volunteers showed up to pile sandbags at the entrance to the Bob Devaney Sports Center in Lincoln when flooding was threatened along nearby Antelope Creek in July 1993.

ROBYNN TYSVER/Lincoln Journal-Star

Sandbags — and miles of mud — were what remained in the Whitetail Lake subdivision near Columbus when the spring floodwaters of 1993 finally receded.

TED KIRK/Lincoln Journal-Star

A 1950s John Deere Model B tractor was mired in a washout caused by the floodwaters that washed through the Thomas Lakes area north of Ashland in March 1993.

RANDY HAMPTON/Lincoln Journal-Star

ROBERT BECKER/Lincoln Journal-Star

ABOVE: The lines of an ancient hay rake stood in stark beauty against a fresh-fallen snow and glowing sky in January 1993. LEFT: But when the early-morning windchill approaches 30 below zero, as it did just a month later, experienced Nebraskans know enough to bundle up tight.

RANDY HAMPTON/Lincoln Journal-Star

ABOVE: Everybody lends a hand when it's time to clear the snow off Lincoln sidewalks. RIGHT: An icy storm, like this one in January 1991, leaves the Capital City beautifully sparkling, but the sidewalks treacherous.

ROBERT BECKER/Lincoln Journal-Star

RANDY HAMPTON/Lincoln Journal-Star

During those few weeks each year when the calendar says it's spring but winter seems to linger on, even Mother Nature isn't always certain which way to go in Nebraska.

"People everywhere read with deep interest the story of the heroism of these school-teachers. Thousands of dollars were raised by the newspapers to reward them and to care for other victims," Sheldon wrote.

It was poorly constructed schools and insufficient fuel for heat that forced teachers to leave their buildings, wrote Ora Clement. "The teacher had no choice but to find other shelter for her charges. Hundreds of little ones were trapped, along with their teachers, in situations where their lives depended on cool judgement and prompt action." Only a few weeks after the blizzard, a letter went out from the state superintendent of schools requesting that all rural schools have their winter supply of fuel under cover before cold weather began each fall.

Clement filled out the story of Minnie Freeman, still in her teens at the time of her heroism. Before she led her 16 pupils out of the sodhouse school building, she had decided they would all spend the night there. But the roaring wind broke the leather hinges of the door and brought it inside. The older boys nailed the door shut, but then a sudden gust caught a corner of the tarpaper roof and ripped it off, leaving a hole through which snow began to drift. Miss Freeman had no option but to strike out in the storm.

Not all pupils were as lucky as Miss Freeman's.

In Dodge County, two sisters, 13 and 8 years old, started from a schoolhouse together. Their widowed mother watched for them anxiously, but they never arrived. Their bodies were found lying together in a field, drifted over with snow. The older girl had taken off her wraps and put them around her little sister.

The pathos of their story was told in print, orally and even in verse, the last lines of which are:

Search in western song and story, and discover if you can,
Braver, grander, nobler action in the history of man;
Than the silent heroism of the child, who, in her woe,
Wrapped her cloak about her sister, as she struggled through the snow.

Livestock, too, fell before the rampage.

In Colfax County at the Omaha Ranch, when the blinding snow descended, frightened cattle stampeded, breaking down gates and fences. Some 250 head froze to death that night, as well as a large percentage of 600 hogs that were being fed there.

After the storm, ranch manager Thomas Mortimer went in search of other cattle who had been pastured away from ranch buildings. When he got to Butterfly Creek, he discovered 60 head of cattle frozen in the ice.

The cold continued through the rest of January and February, making it

Journal-Star Files

In its aftermath, a snowstorm is not without a certain stark beauty — as in this photo taken at a Lincoln park in December 1973.

extremely difficult to find stock, although drifts as high as haystacks supported the weight of searchers. In late February, Mortimer and neighboring rancher John Borland were out walking over such drifts when they noticed steam rising from a snow-covered haystack. Under that haystack were 70 hogs that had been imprisoned there for six weeks. As the hogs died of starvation, the remaining ones fed on their bodies.

If Plains people and their descendants have a toughness, a resiliency not found everywhere, the Blizzard of '88 may have been a factor. Clement believed that the blizzard probably changed the minds of many Easterners of less sterner stuff who were toying with the idea of tackling the frontier. But it strengthened and solidified the state. "It winnowed out the weaklings," she wrote. "Those who made their decision to stay began to think in terms of permanence. This decision led to home and school construction improvement and a growing community interest."

While the blizzards of 1888 and 1949 were predominant, for those who lived through them the battering storms that went before and those that came later carried just as much intensity. There's nothing like being there to feel the bite of the wind and snow and the numbing temperatures.

"Is the measure of a natural hazard a subjective factor that can only be related to personal experience? Ultimately the intensity of such a hazard can be measured only by its rather inestimable impact on each individual who has to cope with and adapt to its exigencies," Lawson wrote.

To the pioneer, blizzards descended without warning and brought fear, sorrow, loss, cold and hunger.

There were few settlers back during the big blows of 1856 and 1873. In 1856 most of them stuck close to the Missouri River; Nebraska City was the largest town in the state. The stories of that blizzard were kept alive by oral reporting, diaries and letters sent back East, where the more civilized found it hard to believe that wolves were chasing deer through the streets of Nebraska City. Settlers as well as wolves found food hard to come by and many would have died had it not been for the game whose mobility was curtailed by the snowdrifts. The crust of snow would bear the weight of humans, but large game with sharp hooves found themselves helpless. One settler was reported to have killed 70 deer, elk and antelope — with an ax.

The Oregon Trail between Nebraska's Fort Kearny and Fort Laramie in Wyoming was covered with two feet of snow, with the valleys and ravines filled with drifts from October until May.

While that whole winter of 1856-57 was blasted with one snowstorm after another, the first real blizzard began on Dec. 1 with rain from the southwest that switched to the northwest and then became fiercely cold. The storm lasted three days, and one writer of the time wrote: "A terrible cold set in on Dec. 1, 1856, freezing into 90 solid blocks of ice all the days of December, January and February."

December is blizzard season and they can be expected then. But the blizzard of 1873 was more surprising than most.

It had been raining on Easter Sunday, April 13, when just before dark the wind changed from the southwest to the northwest and the rain became sleet and the sleet became snow. By Monday morning that snow was being driven with such force that it was impossible to face it, Sheldon wrote. Dugouts, soddies and stables soon were buried, and many cows, pigs and chickens luxuriated in their owners' quarters until the storm passed. Many died in this storm, and although every county had its casualties, no perfect record ever surfaced.

One of the oft-told tragedies of the Easter blizzard concerns a Mrs. Cooper and her two daughters, Emma and Lizzie, who lived in Howard County about 10 miles from St. Paul. They were home alone and Mrs. Cooper, who was not well, went to bed early on Easter night. The two girls sat up, keeping the fire going in the fireplace. The wind blasts increased until an especially tenacious one blew the door open, scattered the coals and set the house ablaze. While the two girls beat the flames out, another blast took the roof off, leaving them in darkness with the house filling with snow.

Journal-Star Files

The blizzard that brought eastern Nebraska to a standstill in January 1975, came as a total surprise to Lincoln bicycle riders.

The mother and daughters huddled through the night under all the bedding they had. By morning, the snow was so deep the girls crawled over the house's walls and headed for a neighbor's home about a mile away to get help for their mother.

As soon as the girls left their house, they lost their way. All day they wandered in the storm, the snow cutting at their faces. They came upon a dugout and beat on its locked door, but only potatoes were stored inside. They didn't know they were within a few yards of the house they were searching for. As night fell, they scooped a hole in the snow and held each other close for warmth. In the morning, Emma tried to rouse her sister by rubbing her hands and face, but Lizzie fell over exhausted and died in the snow with Emma watching over her.

Emma kept walking for 24 more hours, knowing if she stopped she would die. On Wednesday the sun came out and she was within shouting distance of the house she had been trying to reach. The neighbors brought her in and she survived. They later found her mother's body a short distance from the

RANDY HAMPTON/Lincoln Journal-Star

Businesses closed and workers were sent home at midday — before city buses stopped running — when a blizzard struck Lincoln in January 1975.

Cooper home.

Historical accounts cause one to wonder: Did little boys never die in blizzards?

People still die in blizzards, with the 1975 storm claiming 14 lives in Nebraska. While the blizzard of 1949 crippled the western two-thirds of the state, the 1975 blizzard turned the tables, hitting eastern Nebraska, Lincoln and Omaha with full force and toning down its rage over the western half of the state.

The blizzard of 1975 lasted only 24 hours but brought eastern Nebraska to a total standstill. "Weather conditions on Jan. 9 read as if they had come out of a meteorology textbook chapter titled, 'Blizzards'," Lawson wrote. It was warm, moist air from the Gulf of Mexico tangling with a polar air mass from the frigid north that created the storm. On Jan. 10, snow started falling and by midday all routes to Lincoln were blocked. As the snow diminished, the wind kicked up a howl with gusts to 60 mph. Visibility was zero. The storm became an official blizzard the next morning when tempera-

DEAN TERRILL/Lincoln Journal-Star

A winter wonderland of ice-coated trees and fences was the backdrop for these perplexed cattle after a Thanksgiving storm at Burchard in 1983.

tures stood at 10 degrees.

Restaurants, motels and hospitals took in stranded motorists, schools closed, meetings were canceled and all normal public activity was put on hold while the great white visitor held sway.

Nobody has seen wolves chasing deer down the streets in Nebraska City lately, but during the blizzard of January 1975, coyotes had easy pickings on weakened cattle stuck in the snowbanks.

While motorized vehicles strip storms of their potency, sometimes the opposite is true. In 1975, road crews could not work because of stalled vehicles along roadways. United Press International photographer Tom Peterson counted 27 disabled semi-tractor trailers on the 50-mile stretch between Omaha and Lincoln.

There are so many noteworthy winter storms that it is hard to know where to stop their flow. As one example, a Lincoln Star editorial writer claimed that to skip the blizzard of 1971 would be too soon. That writer called for the record books to be reopened for the storm that struck on Jan. 3, 1971. "The 14 inches of snow that fell were whipped by a tremendous wind into a howling blizzard. Drifts piled up to eight and 10 feet deep, and life across eastern Nebraska came to a standstill. The Monday Star, published by a thin skeletal staff Sunday night, had not been delivered to homes by midday.

"In total, it was a winter attack by nature that left the population reeling. We have had more snow accummulation from past storms but certainly no more damaging storm."

The challenges faced from storms spaced over 136 years in time differ greatly. But these things remain constant:

■ Plains blizzards are as dependable as bindweed in their return.

■ They come to remind us that we are impotent before nature's unleashed power.

■ People who were strangers become a true community as they take in the stranded, share their meager supplies and become heroes and heroines superceding their physical limitations in an attempt to save others.

■ No matter how cold or deep it gets, the natural optimism of Plains people remains intact.

Surveying 25-foot snowdrifts that kept him imprisoned on his central Nebraska farm for weeks in 1949, a farmer who had experienced a considerable amount of deprivation greeted his rescuers with a broad grin. "Think of the moisture we'll have for next year's crops when this stuff melts," he said.

Journal-Star Files

FLOODS

"The weather was dry and intensely hot for several weeks, and then, at the end of July, thunderstorms and torrential rains broke upon Sweet Water Valley. The river burst out of its banks, all the creeks were up and the stubble of Ivy Peters' wheat fields lay under water. A wide lake and two rushing creeks now separated the Forresters from town."

— Willa Cather
A Lost Lady

Flash flooding in May 1965 left the streets and sidewalks of Louisville covered with muddy slime — and the National Weather Bureau warned there was still more rain ahead.

FLOODS

Some are simple and homey: Table, Turkey, Timber, Salt, Shell, Rock. Others beg that the stories of their names be told: Dead Man's Run, Weeping Water, Medicine, Dead Horse. They are the arteries that feed the major waterways of the Platte, the Little and Big Blues, the Snake, the Loup, the Little and Big Nemaha, the Niobrara, the Republican and the Missouri rivers. There are more than 1,300 stream names registered in Nebraska.

They most often run at a trickle — sometimes bone dry — and that's why when a sudden local rainstorm or when one upstream fills their banks, overflows and turns their usual placidity into turbulence, the surprise becomes shock.

Between June 12 and June 16, 1990, local rain gauges registered rainfall between 16 and 23 inches at Platte Center. The rain turned Shell Creek, which ordinarily can be jumped — or at least waded — into a mile-wide violent turbo. Bales of hay, timber, propane tanks and automobiles rode the crest toward the Shell's confluence with the Platte, already out of its banks. Retired farmer Elmer Herde stood in awe of the sight, as Lincoln's Sunday Journal-Star reported on June 24, 1990.

Herde had lived beside the Shell's banks for 72 years. "Sometimes it's almost dry," he said. But for the first time in its history, the stream began inching toward the Herde farm buildings, then rented out. With 3,600 bushels of soybeans in storage the decision was made to move the crop to Wagner Mills in Schuyler. The beans that were left behind got wet, swelled and pushed the sides out of the granary. It was also necessary to move 5,000 bushels of corn. "We also lost 150 acres of row crops. The field is so covered with debris and silt that we're done for this year," Herde said. "I've never seen the Shell like this. I'm disappointed in it."

Journal-Star Files

Ending a devastating drought with a vengeance, the Republican River flood of May 1935 left this twisted wreckage where a railroad had run only days before.

Part of the disappointment felt from the major elements of Nebraska's weather is its senseless inconsistencies. While 1990 was a weather year to remember — with excessive rainfall running wild — at the same time, a state climatology statistician said, "We are still short of moisture in the subsoil. The recharge from previous (dry) years is still missing."

But that was nothing compared to the irony of the Great Flood of 1935. The state was in the middle of a devastating drought when rains started falling in the Republican River Valley in May 1935. By May 20, it seemed the back of the drought had been broken for the southern tier of Nebraska counties. Not only was the ground saturated in Dundy, Hitchcock, Red Willow, Furnas, Harlan, Franklin, Frontier, Webster and Nuckolls counties, the Republican River had been out of its banks those last days of the month.

The river finally subsided, and the smiles created by having survived the drought quickly changed to shrieks of despair when cloudbursts in northeastern Colorado turned both the South Platte and then the Republican into raging torrents. Nobody knows how much rain fell, but the estimate was 24 inches in a 24-hour period.

A never forgotten symbol of that ravaging flood was the body of Mary Thomas, found hanging in a tree 75 miles downstream and three weeks after the Thomases' Trenton home caved in under the turbulent water. Her husband, Jim, and son, Spencer, were never found.

The missing make the number of fatalities hard to pinpoint, but 112 deaths is close. A baby drowned at Parks, and the Taylor family of four at Benkelman disappeared and were never found. The J.R. Pettit family — eight members — were drowned. Orville Fuchs of Oxford lost his wife, mother and daughter, all clinging to the rooftop of their farmhouse as it was swept away. Fuchs reportedly walked the river banks for days, searching, hoping to find the bodies.

The story of the men trying to save the Nebraska Light and Power plant in south McCook is the stuff of which movies are made.

A sandbag crew of 37 was trapped by rising water. To save themselves they took to the roof, but the power of the rushing water made rescue by boat impossible. Attempting to use utility poles as a means of escape, a large rope was strung between a pole nearest the plant and a pole on shore by an heroic Paul Wilson, who shinnied along the electric wires to string the

Journal-Star Files

A sandbag crew struggling to protect the Nebraska Light and Power plant at McCook clung to its broken roof as the Republican River rose, stranding them overnight.

line. The plan was to attach a pulley to the rope and tow each man to safety. Two were rescued that way, but then the poles caved into the raging waters — water then ate away at the power plant, first taking down a standpipe on the side of the building. Finally the building itself sagged and the roof collapsed in the middle as its steel frame buckled. The remaining men clung to what was left of the roof all night. The next day, all were ferried to safety.

According to the McCook Gazette, by June 3, 1935, in addition to the dead, 68 people had been injured, 121 homes destroyed and 320 damaged; 146 barns and 913 other buildings were gone, and hundreds more had been damaged. Additionally, 258 horses, 2,228 head of cattle and 71,000 poultry had drowned or disappeared. Forty miles of the Burlington Railroad's main line had to be rebuilt. And 250,000 acres of some of the richest farmland in the state had been rendered useless by silt, debris and erosion.

One account of the surprise attack of the roaring Republican was told by Warren Spencer, writing in the June 1971 edition of NebraskaLand magazine:

Sidney Clawson was a hired man who worked for Victor Saylor. The two had settled down to talk after dinner, but at about 9 p.m. a deafening roar shattered their peaceful evening. Both scrambled for the door and burst into the front yard. To their amazement, Spencer wrote, a large barn was floating away on an unbelievable flood tide. The usually shallow Republican River was suddenly more than four miles wide, according to the historical marker west of Oxford, and 20 to 25 feet deep in some places.

Clawson went back to the house, grabbed the youngest child and swam toward a tree. With the tot still clinging to him, Clawson was almost immediately washed downstream. This happened twice more until they were able to latch on to a large tree. The man and child were there for 36 hours before they were rescued by boat.

Nebraskans never stand so tall as when they pull tragedy inside out, vow "never again" and act on that pledge. Flood control of the Republican River Valley became a crusade for Harry Strunk, publisher of the McCook Daily Gazette. The result of that commitment incorporated the federal Pick-Sloan Plan (Pick was the blizzard buster of 1949) for flood control throughout the Missouri River Valley into the Republican River watershed. As a result, six dams were built — one in Colorado and five in Nebraska. They include the Strunk across Medicine Creek northwest of Cambridge; the Enders on Frenchman Creek; the Harlan and Trenton on the Republican, and the Red Willow on Red Willow Creek, north of McCook.

Because of the lives and property lost, the Republican River flood of 1935 stands as one of the state's greatest tragedies, but Nebraska State Historical Society records tell the story of an earlier flood at the very same time

Nebraska State Historical Society

Omaha's smelting plant became an island when rapid snow melt swelled the Missouri River in the spring of 1881.

of the year in that very same watershed.

Army Capt. Alex Moore reported to his commanding officer of the Department of the Platte that while patroling the Republican Valley, on Blackwood Creek, May 29, 1873: "A terrible freshet without warning and apparent cause swept down the valley, carrying everything before it; men, horses, tents, army wagons were swept away like corks. For five days we had no rain and how this water came so suddenly, I cannot yet understand.

"The valley of the Blackwood is about 45 miles long (it enters the Republican about two miles east of Culbertson) and about one mile to a half wide. The entire stretch of country was one raging torrent, at least six to seven feet deep, and how any man or horse escaped is marvelous. . . . When day broke the morning of June 1, it showed almost all the men of my campany in tree tops and without any covering except remanants of underclothing and beneath them the torrent still raging. . . . The settlers at the mouth of the Blackwood lost almost all their stock and property. Six of my company were drowned and 26 horses lost.

"I remained at the scene of the disaster for four days and received five of

Nebraska State Historical Society

The town of Niobrara, situated at the confluence of the Niobrara and Missouri rivers, got a double dose when waters rose in March 1881.

the bodies of the men and almost all the equipment of my command."

The sixth body was found much later.

It was not only the Republican River whose waters could not be corraled. People living along all Nebraska rivers and many of its creeks are no strangers to water's devastating power.

The winter of 1880-81 had unusual snowfall. Trains could not run, mail deliveries stopped and farmers found that just taking care of their livestock took every daylight hour. During the last week in March, the weather turned warm and snow melted rapidly, according to State Historical Society records. Creeks and rivers filled with water and overflowed, and ice in the streams broke loose, tearing away everything in its path.

After every watercourse in Nebraska was full and overflowing, the snow melt began in the Dakotas, pouring still more water into the swollen Missouri River. On the night of March 29, 1881, water began to rise in the town of Niobrara, located at the confluence of the Niobrara and Missouri rivers. It covered the first floors of houses, cellars were filled and much furniture and household goods were ruined.

To avert future problems, the following summer the entire town was moved to a plateau about 20 feet above the flood plain.

Nebraska State Historical Society

Vowing to beat the dangerous power of Nebraska's common spring floods, the people of Niobrara jacked up their entire community and moved it a mile and a half west — and 20 feet above the flood plain — in the summer of 1881.

Journal-Star Files

Flooding of Salt Creek in 1908 left rail cars stranded in the Burlington yards at Lincoln.

Journal-Star Files

Lincoln streets were awash in floodwaters, but residents of tiny Ashland faced the real danger after a 5-inch rain swelled Salt Creek in 1908.

A little downstream, Green Island, a village of 150 people, found the Missouri River rising on March 30. On the following day the ice jam above the village broke, and while Green Islanders watched from across the river on rooftops in Yankton, S.D., their houses, businesses, cattle, horses, uprooted trees and everything else that makes up a town rushed off down the Missouri River. Within two hours, Green Island, except for one house, had been swept away.

"When ice jams melt, everything that they have been holding up comes downstream in an uncontrolled rush," said KMTV meteorologist Carey Coleman. "It is a perpetual problem in a climate cold enough to freeze rivers."

In 1908, with rain-swollen Rock and Wahoo creeks running bankful, residents of Ashland were warned to vacate because a 5-inch rain that had just

Journal-Star Files

Flooding in May 1950, described as the worst in Nebraska since 1908, swept the Burlington Railroad tracks between Palmyra and Syracuse right off their roadbed.

fallen at Lincoln was rolling down Salt Creek, headed in their direction. Only a few heeded the warning. "By midnight it (Salt Creek) was out of its banks, a little later the fire bell was rung and firearms woke the slumbering citizens," according to the Ashland Gazette.

A young man, Guy Hooker, became a hero of that flood, as "he went where others dared not go, seemingly into the very jaws of death, his boat being rocked and tossed by violent waves." Hooker, whose age was not reported in the news story but who was said to look like a teen-ager, rescued families from roofs of houses and from treetops. Only one life was lost, but "there is not a house that is not severely damaged in some way. Some of them are mere wrecks. There is scarcely a small barn, stable or out-building left standing. Several horses were drowned, and the loss of pigs, chickens and other animals was nearly total."

Too often and everywhere, floods have disrupted lives across Nebraska. On June 22, 1947, a flood flashed down Medicine Creek into Cambridge, taking 13 lives and leaving the town of 1,000 clogged with mud, muck and debris.

In May 1950, it was if a cloud had been unzipped to drop its contents in southeastern Nebraska; 7 inches of rain fell quickly, turning the Big Blue and Nemaha rivers into tumultuous water roller coasters.

"Worst flood since 1908," officials said.

Twenty-two people lost their lives and five were missing and presumed drowned.

A Burlington Lines bus was washed off of Nebraska 2 between Syracuse and Unadilla where Wolf Creek crosses the highway, carrying several passengers to a watery death. One passenger survived after drifting four miles downstream where she caught hold of the top of a tree and where she spent the night. The bus was found in the Little Nemaha River about 2½ miles from Nebraska 2. Several people died when their cars were swept off U.S. 77 south of Lincoln.

Railroad tracks and bridges of the Union Pacific, Burlington and Rock Island railroads were torn loose and washed away. The North 10th Street bridge that spanned Salt Creek in Lincoln was swept downstream. The west edge of the Capital City was a huge lake, and the Red Cross set up a shelter at Park School in Lincoln to house those whose homes in both the North and South Bottoms neighborhoods were under water.

Total damage was estimated at $53 million — $308.46 million in 1994 dollars.

Just two months later, on July 8, a 13-inch rainfall at York sent the Blue River and its tributaries all over the countryside. Five lives were lost near Fullerton and property damage was again in the millions. That rainfall is the largest amount ever recorded in the state in one 24-hour period, according to David Ludlum in *The American Weather Book.* Tecumseh holds the record for the greatest monthly accumulation of 20 inches during June 1883; Omaha holds title for a year's total of 64.5 inches during 1969.

The loss of life, damage to farmlands — some farms lost as much as 4 inches of topsoil — and property damage to towns by those floods of 1950 were the driving force that created the Salt-Wahoo watershed. Spearheaded by Lincoln Journal Editor Raymond A. McConnell Jr. — and with the active support of dairy farmer and state Sen. Otto H. Liebers, Gov. Robert B. Crosby and many others — for 10 years the organization pushed and prodded legislation through the U.S. Congress that resulted in corralling the floodwaters that repeatedly decimated farms and towns in the 1,627 square miles, covering more than a million acres of the watershed. The organization changed its name to the Salt Valley Watershed in 1960 after Wahoo dropped out of the effort.

Noting that between 1900 and 1952, 136 floods — 22 of major proportion — occurred in the watershed and to keep rain on the land where it falls, the Salt Valley effort included the straightening of channels, the construction of small farm ponds and the addition of 10 larger water-retaining structures built by the U.S. Army Corps of Engineers. Those later structures are known to boaters and fishermen today as the Salt Valley lakes: Wagon Train, Conestoga, Bluestem, Olive Creek, Stagecoach, Branched Oak, Pawnee, Yankee Hill, Twin and Holmes Park.

During the floods of 1993, the dams built in the 1950s made a whole lot of difference. "Virtually all the news coverage about the floods of 1993 has been about what went wrong. The thousands of earth retention dams that Nebraska has been putting in place on river tributaries since the 1950s appear to be among the things that went right," Lincoln's Sunday Journal-Star reported on Aug. 1, 1993.

The organized watersheds across the state evolved into Natural Resources Districts; Nebraska is the only state in the nation having such a system.

Those Nebraskans who wept at the telecasts of the valiant efforts of men, women and children along the Mississippi River during the summer of 1993, as they fought to hold back the floodwaters from their towns, may not have been old enough to remember — or old enough to have forgotten — the battle the city of Omaha fought against the Mighty Mo in 1952. The city won.

In 1950, Civil Defense was an urgent national program. The rush to build state, local and national organizations bordered on an hysterical fear of atomic war, wrote Sam Reynolds in the April 16, 1972, edition of the Omaha World-Herald's Magazine of the Midlands.

It is universally true that if you have troops geared for battle, they lust for a fight. The trained and ready Civil Defense organization in Omaha got to test its battle plan when Gen. Don G. Shingler, Missouri River chief of engineers, warned Nebraska's largest city that the greatest flood in the history of the white man was coming downstream.

In *Roundup: A Nebraska Reader,* B.F. Sylvester described that flood's approach: "Big Mo was roaring drunk on a snow-melt cocktail which could have been mixed by Paul Bunyan. It was made in Montana and the Dakotas

Journal-Star Files

The devastating Missouri River flood of 1952 left hundreds of farms and fields inaccessible from Omaha north to South Sioux City.

Journal-Star Files

When the Blue River, swollen with heavy spring rains, began rising in 1967, residents of Crete turned out to pile sandbags in the street.

Journal-Star Files

Its moat looking like a lake within a lake, the Stuhr Museum at Grand Island stood isolated by Platte River flooding in 1967, protected only by the high road that ringed it.

with 80 thousand square miles of deep winter snow which was one-third water, a chinook wind, and an almost total runoff over a layer of ice. . . . An unprecedented volume rolled over towns and farms for a thousand miles into a bottleneck at Omaha and Council Bluffs."

The flood stage of the Missouri River at Omaha at that time was 26½ feet. The flood of 1952 crested at 40 feet and was funneled past the city only by the heroic efforts of 35,000 volunteers who filled and placed millions of sandbags. Eighteen miles of dikes, levees and flood walls were raised four to five feet higher in a matter of six days. The Civil Defense effort included the Red Cross, Salvation Army, U.S. Army, Air Force, Coast Guard, Navy, National Guard, the local police force and the Civil Air Patrol. It included students from Creighton University, the University of Omaha, the University of Nebraska; women with coffee and sandwiches; 180 radio hams who flocked in from all over the nation, and young girls who freed up adult flood fighters by caring for others' children. During the greatest threat, citizens living in the flood plain of both Omaha and Council Bluffs were evacuated.

While it was nip and tuck at times, the hastily built dikes held and victory was declared on April 20.

National radio newsman Edward R. Murrow included the effort in a newscast: "Civil Defense had both plans and leaders. It's like an army. If you have a staff together with company and squad leaders, when thousands of recruits arrive, you can do something. It may not be good but you can get going. That's what happened here. . . . People who live along this section of the Missouri have gained a certain dignity from their fight with the river and set an example of fortitude and hardiness."

But water does not disappear. It keeps rolling along, and the whole Missouri River Valley downstream — towns and farmland — were under thousands of acre-feet of water. When it arrived at Rulo, it was 8.6 feet above Rulo's 17-foot flood stage — a record yet to be broken.

"As moving water becomes deeper, it tends to run faster. Gravity causes water to run downhill, while friction against a stream's bed and banks tend to hold it back," as reported in *USA Today Weather*. "The water's speed depends on a balance between gravity and friction. As a stream becomes wider or deeper, a smaller share of the water is rubbing against the banks or bed. The gravity-friction balance then tilts more toward gravity and the water speeds up."

Sometimes Nebraska floods have their origins thousands of miles away.

El Nino is a warming of waters in the western Pacific Ocean, a long way from the Plains, but that warming brings a whole lot of weight to bear on Nebraska. Prevailing winds blow the warm water east, where it generates wide areas of thunderstorms in the eastern Pacific. Those storms disrupt the jet stream in the Northern Hemisphere, according to The Associated

HUMBERTO RAMIREZ/Lincoln Journal-Star

After flooding in July 1984, heavy timbers and debris jammed a bridge on Highway 2 at Lincoln.

MICHAEL HOLMES/Lincoln Journal-Star

A bridge on U.S. Highway 77 south of Wahoo was nearly blocked by rising floodwaters in September 1977.

Press. Rain-producing clouds, which usually would be carried away be the jet stream, just get stuck on hold. And drop rain and more rain.

Normally, the warming process happens twice during a decade and lasts 12 to 18 months. The current El Nino began in 1991 and was slated to end in July 1992, but it is now almost 3 years old and heating up again. Gerald Bell, a National Oceanic and Atmospheric Administration meteorologist with the Climate Analysis Center in Washington, D.C., blames the current El Nino for the Midwest floods of 1993. And although not all meteorologists agree with Bell, he is hoisting the flood signals for 1994.

The extent of flooding in southeast Nebraska in 1993 can best be described by flood stages and crests as reported in The Lincoln Star:

- Ashland: Salt Creek flood stage, 16 feet; crest on July 23 at 23 feet.
- Auburn: Little Nemaha flood stage, 22 feet; crest on July 24 at 26.6 feet.
- Beatrice: Big Blue flood stage, 16 feet; crest on July 26 at 28.8 feet.

■ Greenwood: Salt Creek flood stage, 20 feet; crest on July 24 at 26.5 feet.

■ Louisville: Platte River flood stage, 9 feet; crest on July 23 at 12.2 feet.

■ Nebraska City: Missouri River flood stage, 18 feet, crest on July 23 at 27.2 feet.

■ Rulo: Missouri River flood stage, 17 feet; crest on July 24 at 25.3 feet.

Those over-flood-stage crests represent a whole lot of houses, farms and businesses inundated with water; tons of silt and muck left behind; and people losing a lifetime's work and savings. Fifty-two Nebraska counties were eligible for federal disaster aid after the floods of 1993.

Not only were the river levels at record highs, but the flood of 1993 was unusual because of its timing, Coleman said. "Most major Midwest floods occur during the late winter or early spring. Summer is not a normal time for these great floods."

In a more perfect world, Nebraska's floods and droughts would be leveled out so that human endeavors might reasonably be hitched to efforts other than dealing with nature's whims. But then would Nebraskans have to built up their mental muscles by deliberately finding other, tougher hills to climb?

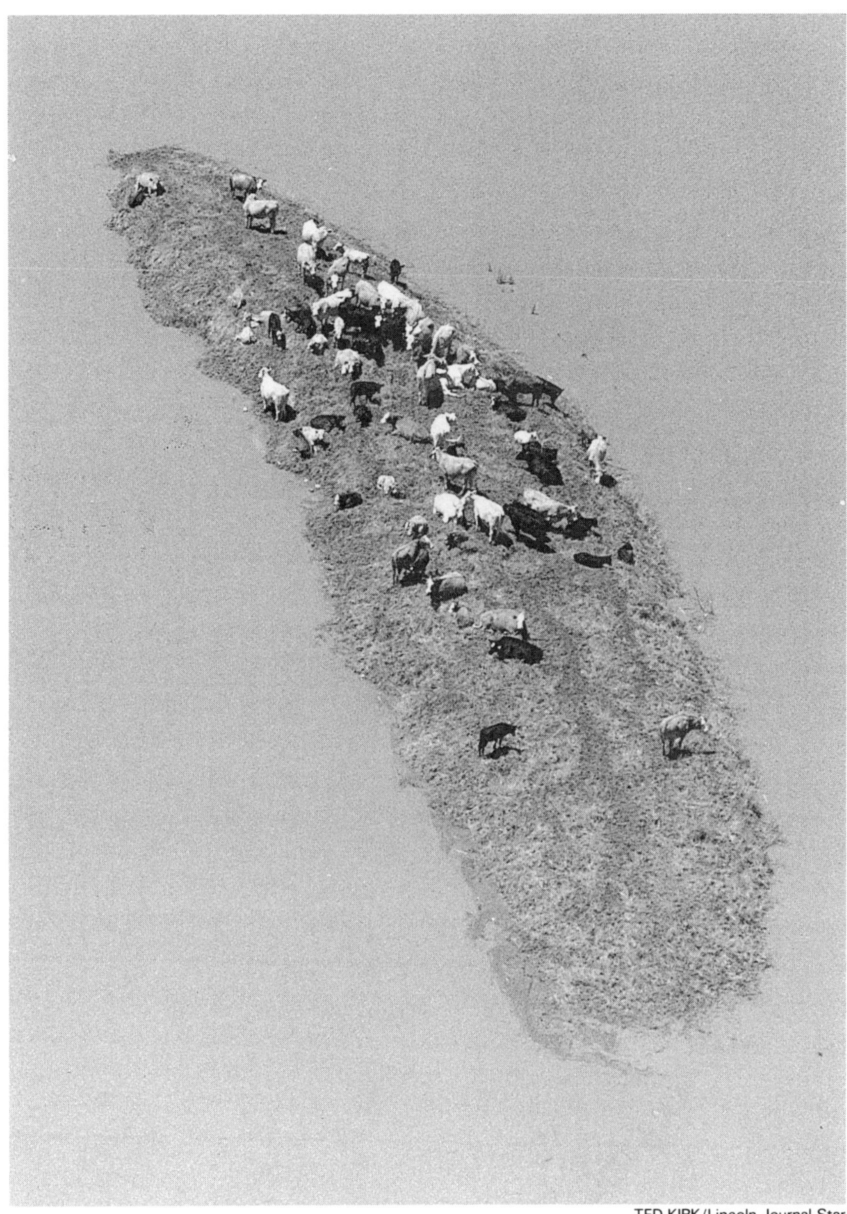

TED KIRK/Lincoln Journal-Star

Platte River flooding, brought on when especially heavy winter snow cover and a quick spring thaw combined forces in 1993, left this small herd of cattle huddled on the high ground.

HARALD DREIMANIS/Lincoln Journal-Star

A brilliant bolt of lightning, flashing high into the clouds, brightened downtown Lincoln in 1982.

THE EVOLUTION OF FORECASTING

Weather forecasting began with observations like Benjamin Franklin's that storms not only are localized events but actually move over space and time. With the simple realization that weather systems were traveling events, forecasting suddenly made sense as a worthwhile scientific endeavor. With Newton's mechanics — gravitation, motion, chemical composition, temperature — in hand, weather scientists were able to mathematically describe the motions of the atmosphere once they started getting the necessary data.

The oldest continuous upper-air observing station in the Free World was established in Omaha in 1898. Initially, kites were used to collect information. After using manned balloons and airplanes to gather data, the first radio-transmitting weather balloons were used in Omaha in July 1938, as a network of Radiosondes Stations was established across the country. That data was then, and still is, the very basis for weather forecasting in North America.

The data explosion began in earnest with aviation. When pilots took to the skies they saw first-hand what was really happening in the atmosphere at great heights.

With higher flying planes during World War II, the jet stream was discovered. Once this dynamic, upper-level river of air had been identified, its relationship to ground-level weather was established, and it became the backbone of the computer modeling that is the basis of most of the forecasting done in the world today. As the importance of dynamics became known and forecastable, many different computer models evolved with a great deal of accuracy.

Today we have observations from land, sea, air and space. It was the advent of weather satellites in the 1960s that allowed a quantum leap in forecasting major weather systems. This added to the vast radar network that already had been established through much of the United States during the 1950s.

The next great advance in weather observation has come through development of Doppler radar. Television stations and research facilities have been using Doppler radar for more than a decade. Simply put, Doppler beams hit raindrops and measure both their speed and direction. That shows the rotating motion in a thunderstorm, which gives warning lead time.

The National Weather Service is now setting up a Doppler network called Nexrad. One such station under construction at Valley, Neb., is to be completed in 1994 and will consolidate weather reporting operations currently stationed in Omaha, Lincoln, Norfolk and Sioux City, Iowa. These are powerful tools for detecting actual winds within thunderstorms, including tornadoes. During severe weather, proper use of Doppler permits warning of tornadoes more than half an hour in advance.

Using the Doppler principle, a device called a profiler is now being used to detect the winds in the upper atmosphere. Radiosondes are taken twice a day around the country simultaneously, but profilers can take measurements through the day or night, and their widescale use is expected to lead to improved forecasting.

While storms often still do strike without warning, warnings are getting better every day with modern technology.

Good reporting, however, does not negate personal responsibility for one's safety during storm conditions.

— Carey Coleman
KMTV meteorologist

Carey Coleman, a native of Illinois, has worked at the Weather Channel, CNN, and radio and television stations from Georgia to Colorado. He came to Omaha TV station KMTV as chief meteorologist in July 1993; his broadcasts also are carried on radio KFAB.

Coleman makes his own weather analyses but keeps no statistics on his accuracy, explaining that the few times he's been wrong have burned themselves into his memory.

AFTERWORD

"Our weather has become much more variable — with more extremes of hot and cold, wet and dry — since about 1980," Dan Atkin said in the December 1993 edition of Reader's Digest. Atkin, a senior meteorologist with the U.S. National Weather Service in San Diego, added that during the last two years our weather has gone crazy.

While Atkin speaks of weather nationwide, the same is true of Nebraska.

"We're recognizing that this (crazy weather) is normal, that the quiet weather of the 1950s and 1960s was the exception. From now on, we should expect the unexpected."

A hot topic in the weather prediction business is the question of whether human activity is changing the Earth's climate. The planet absorbs energy from the Sun and almost the same amount of solar energy flows back into space. When the outflow of heat is blocked by carbon dioxide and other atmospheric gasses, the phenomenon known as the greenhouse effect comes into play. That name comes from its similarity to the way glass panes of a greenhouse trap heat.

Some researchers say we are toying with serious consequences if we do not stop the consumption of fossil fuels, the source of carbon dioxide.

As polar icecaps melt, oceans could rise, landlocked cities could become seaports, seaports would be under water, agricultural lands would produce only dust and hurricanes would be on the increase.

One theory that seems contradictory is that 120,000 years ago the region was as warm as it is today but was plunging into an ice age.

But it isn't really contradictory. "As researchers use sophisticated new tools to probe past climate, the oddly chilling evidence suggests that some past ice ages might not have been triggered by a plunge in temperatures but by a climate similar to today's," Lowell Ponte wrote in Reader's Digest.

Nebraskans, who have been at the mercy of the weather extremes since prehistoric times, don't fret very much about the past or look too far into the future. They usually are much too busy sandbagging their rivers and creeks, praying for rain, jump-starting their cars, salting their sidewalks, shoveling their driveways, pumping out their water-filled basements, repairing their wind-damaged roofs, replanting their washed-out or blown-out crops, chopping their firewood, and breaking holes in the ice of their livestock watering tanks.

"No matter how sophisticated weather reporting is, the science is only about 100 years old, and that is not long enough to make predicting reliable," said KMTV meteorologist Carey Coleman. Weather patterns are far more complicated than giving a lot of credence to the greenhouse effect warrants.

"If the first predictions had been true, we would be having a much hotter, drier climate than we are having," Coleman said.

APPENDICES

NEBRASKA RECORD HIGHS AND LOWS

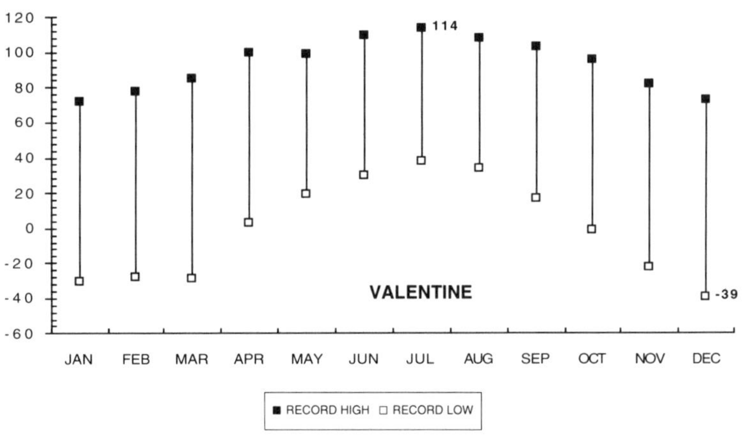

NEBRASKA RECORD HIGHS AND LOWS

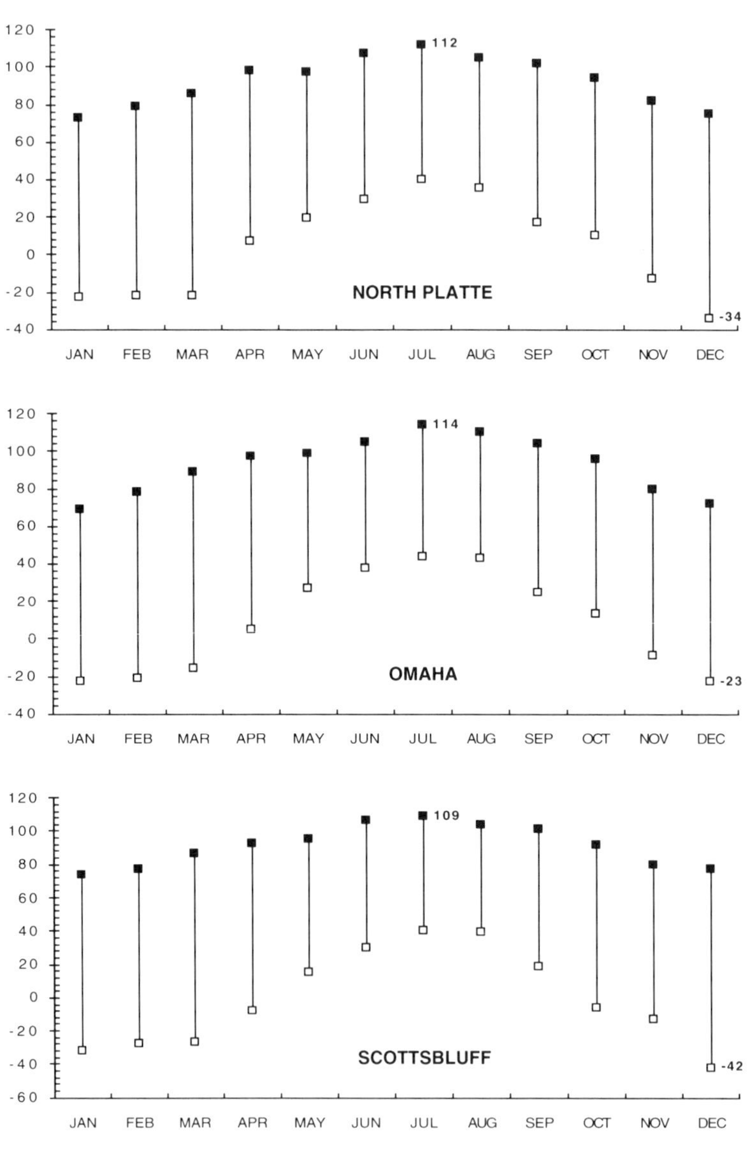

NEBRASKA RECORD HIGHS AND LOWS

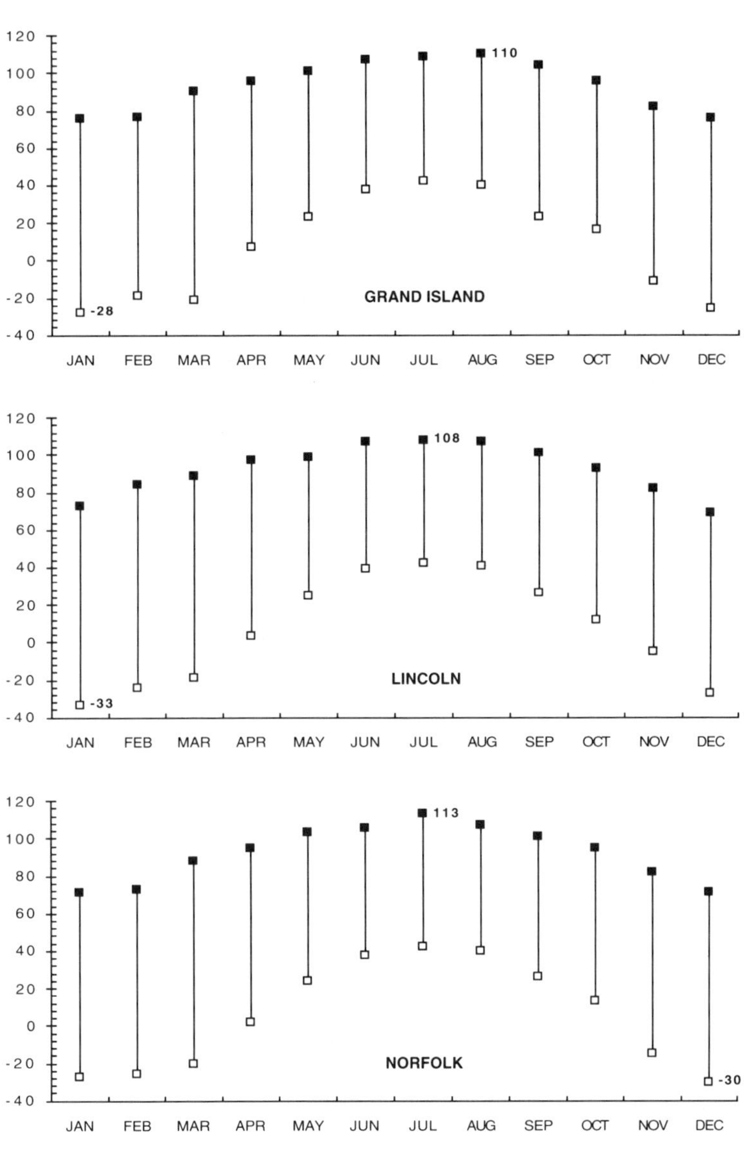

NEBRASKA TEMPERATURE SUMMARY

TOWN/ CITY	JAN AVG HIGH	JAN AVG LOW	JUL AVG HIGH	JUL AVG LOW	RECORD HIGH	MONTH YEAR	RECORD LOW	MONTH YEAR
Ainsworth	32.5	10.4	88.7	61.9	109	Jul-54	-28	Jan-66
Alliance	36.0	10.5	87.1	58.2	109	Jul-54	-33	Dec-64
Beatrice	33.6	13.2	90.6	66.6	114	Jul-54	-21	Jan-74
Broken Bow	35.0	8.8	88.3	60.8	116	Jul-54	-36	Jan-63
Chadron	34.6	9.1	89.4	59.0	110	Jul-54	-29	Dec-78
Columbus	30.0	9.6	88.5	65.0	109	Jul-54	-26	Jan-63
Falls City	34.8	14.6	89.2	66.6	109	Jul-80	-20	Jan-74
Grand Island	31.2	9.9	88.8	64.4	110	Aug-83	-28	Jan-63
Hastings	34.0	12.0	90.0	63.7	110	Jul-54	-19	Jan-74
Kearney	33.0	9.2	88.6	63.7	113	Jul-54	-22	Jan-63
Kimball	38.5	12.6	86.9	56.5	103	Jun-54	-30	Jan-63
Lincoln	30.4	8.9	89.5	65.6	108	Jul-90	-33	Jan-74
McCook	39.5	13.3	91.8	63.8	110	Jul-54	-21	Jan-59
Norfolk	27.8	6.9	87.4	64.2	113	Jul-54	-30	Dec-89
North Platte	34.2	8.3	87.8	60.6	112	Jul-54	-34	Dec-89
Omaha	30.2	10.2	88.5	66.8	114	Jul-36	-23	Dec-89
O'Neill	29.6	7.8	88.5	61.6	110	Jul-54	-31	Dec-67
Scottsbluff	37.2	11.2	89.2	59.2	109	Jul-89	-42	Dec-89
Sidney	37.6	10.9	87.6	56.8	107	Jul-54	-30	Jan-63
Valentine	31.6	5.8	88.7	60.3	114	Jul-90	-39	Dec-89

NEBRASKA PRECIPITATION SUMMARY

TOWN/ CITY	AVG. ANNUAL RAINFALL	AVG. ANNUAL SNOWFALL	REC.MO. RAINFALL	MONTH YEAR	REC.MO. SNOWFALL	MONTH YEAR
Ainsworth	21.87	39.0	10.60	Jul-62	29.0	Nov-72
Alliance	16.83	48.2	7.85	May-57	26.7	Mar-59
Beatrice	30.16	27.6	15.44	Aug-54	27.0	Feb-65
Broken Bow	21.57	30.7	10.33	Jun-65	20.0	Jan-60
Chadron	14.91	42.1	7.96	Jun-67	24.2	Mar-75
Columbus	25.72	26.5	12.49	Jun-67	20.5	Dec-68
Falls City	34.72	24.2	11.02	Sep-59	28.0	Mar-60
Grand Island	23.31	30.3	13.96	Jun-67	26.0	Dec-73
Hastings	27.30	28.4	12.61	Sep-73	31.0	Dec-73
Kearney	24.53	30.4	15.14	Jun-67	23.0	Dec-72
Kimball	17.13	50.8	11.40	May-57	32.0	Mar-59
Lincoln	26.92	27.1	8.57	Aug-82	19.8	Dec-73
McCook	19.85	29.4	7.35	Jun-72	23.5	Mar-52
Norfolk	23.79	30.2	12.22	Jun-67	22.8	Feb-84
North Platte	19.47	30.0	8.01	May-62	21.9	Mar-80
Omaha	30.34	31.0	13.75	Sep-65	27.2	Mar-48
O'Neill	22.83	32.7	9.17	Jul-58	20.7	Dec-68
Scottsbluff	14.59	40.9	8.33	Jun-47	23.7	Jan-49
Sidney	18.29	40.4	10.51	Jun-65	22.2	Apr-58
Valentine	17.11	32.4	8.96	Jul-83	51.0	Mar-77

WIND CHILL INDEX

ACTUAL TEMPERATURE

WIND SPEED (M.P.H.)	40	30	20	10	0	-10	-20	-30	-40	-50
0-4	40	30	20	10	0	-10	-20	-30	-40	-50
5	37	27	16	6	-5	-15	-26	-36	-47	-57
10	28	16	3	-9	-22	-34	-46	-58	-71	-83
15	23	9	-5	-18	-31	-45	-58	-72	-85	-99
20	19	4	-10	-24	-39	-53	-67	-81	-95	-110
25	16	1	-15	-29	-44	-59	-74	-88	-103	-117
30	13	-2	-18	-33	-49	-64	-79	-93	-109	-123
35	12	-4	-20	-35	-52	-67	-82	-97	-113	-128
40	11	-5	-21	-37	-53	-69	-84	-100	-115	-131
45	10	-6	-22	-38	-54	-70	-85	-102	-117	-133

HEAT INDEX (APPARENT TEMPERATURE)

ACTUAL TEMPERATURE

RELATIVE HUMIDITY	70	75	80	85	90	95	100	105	110	115
0	64	69	73	78	83	87	91	95	99	103
10	65	70	75	80	85	90	95	100	105	111
20	66	72	77	82	87	93	99	105	112	120
30	67	73	78	84	90	96	104	113	123	135
40	68	74	79	86	93	101	110	123	137	151
50	69	75	81	88	96	107	120	135	150	
60	70	76	83	90	100	114	132	149		
70	70	77	85	93	106	124	144			
80	71	78	87	97	113	136				
90	71	79	89	102	122					
100	72	80	91	108						

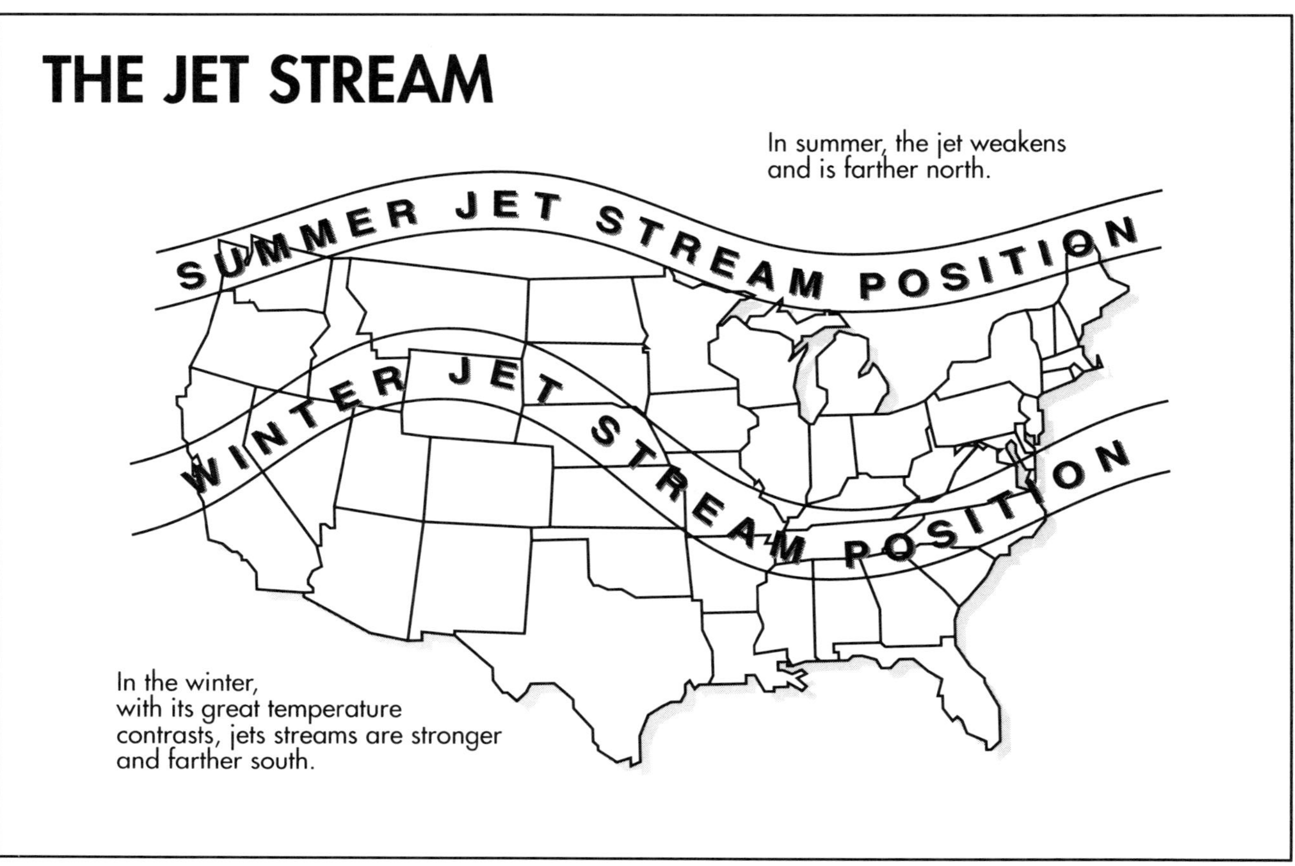
THE JET STREAM
In summer, the jet weakens
and is farther north.
SUMMER JET STREAM POSITION
WINTER JET STREAM POSITION
In the winter,
with its great temperature
contrasts, jets streams are stronger
and farther south.

BIBLIOGRAPHY

BOOKS

American Weather Book, David Ludlum; Houghton Mifflin, 1982.

Climatic Atlas of Nebraska, Kenneth F. Dewey, Merlin P. Lawson, Ralph Neild; University of Nebraska Press, 1977.

Climatography of the United States, No. 20, Nebraska; National Oceanic and Atmospheric Administration

Conquering The Great American Desert, Everett Dick; Nebraska Historical Society, 1975.

Encyclopedia of Earth System Science, D.A. Wilhite; Academic Press, 1992.

History and Stories of Nebraska, A.W. Sheldon; University Publishing Co., 1926.

In All Its Fury, compiled by W.H. O'Gara; Blizzard Club of 1888.

Local Climatological Data, Annual Sumaries for 1992; National Oceanic and Atmospheric Administration

Lightning, Stephen Kramer; Carolrhoda Books, 1992.

Roundup: A Nebraska Reader, compiled by Virginia Faulkner; University of Nebraska Press, 1957.

South of The Cottonwood Tree, Hallie Myers Nelson; Purcell, 1977.

The Violent Earth, Frank W. Lane; Salem House, 1986.

USA Today Weatherbook, Jack Williams; Vintage Books, 1992.

Weather, Ti Sanders; Icarus Press, 1985.

Weather In Your Life, Louis J. Batten; Freeman, 1983.

World of The Wind, Slater Brown; Bobbs-Merrill, 1961.

PERIODICALS

Ashland Gazette
Axtell Republican
Grand Island Independent
McCook Gazette
Lincoln Journal
The Lincoln Star
Lincoln Journal-Star
NEBRASKAland Magazine
Nebraska History Magazine
North Platte Telegraph
Omaha Daily News
Omaha World-Herald
Omaha World-Herald's Magazine of the Midlands
Water International
Weatherwise

ABOUT THE AUTHOR

Betty Stevens entered the writing business as a free-lancer more than 30 years ago when she needed a respite from diaper folding. She began writing a column "Happenings" for the Lincoln Journal in 1968, took over as youth page editor for three years and then became a general assignment reporter.

Needing a respite from all that newspapering, she left in 1977 to run a cowboy saloon in Colorado. Then, believing her education now was complete, she scurried back into newspapering as regional reporter for the Durango (Colo.) Herald, regional reporter for the Verde Independent in Cottonwood, Ariz., and then covered federal agencies, including the 98th Congress, for Prentice-Hall in Washington, D.C.

Life is a circle. She returned to the Durango Herald and then went back to the Lincoln Journal in 1985, where she covered religion before becoming a regional reporter for the Lincoln Journal-Star in 1987. The year 1990 was one of her all-time favorites. Beginning with March 13, every time she looked out the window there was a new tornado or flood to report on. She retired from her daily work in 1992 and now is trying to get all the way back to her beginnings as a free-lancer.